MW00845608

Gartner and the Magic Quadrant:
A Guide For Buyers, Vendors and Investors

Shaun Snapp

Copyrighted Material

Gartner and the Magic Quadrant: A Guide for Buyers, Vendors and Investors

Copyright © 2013 by SCM Focus Press

ALL RIGHTS RESERVED
No part of this publication may be reproduced, stored in a retrieval system or transmitted, in any form or by any means—electronic, mechanical, photocopying, recording or otherwise—without prior written permission, except for the inclusion of brief quotations in a review.

For information about this title or to order other books and/or electronic media, contact the publisher:
SCM Focus Press
PO Box 29502 #9059
Las Vegas, NV 89126-9502
http://www.scmfocus.com/scmfocuspress
(408) 657-0249

ISBN: 978-1-939731-12-8

Printed in the United States of America

Cover and interior design by: 1106 Design

CHAPTER 1

Introduction

Software selection is the most important part of any software implementation because it is the best opportunity to match the software with the business requirements. Doing so goes a long way toward determining the probability of success of the software's future implementation. Once the software selection is made, a number of avenues will be cut off to the company in that the opportunity to change direction or choose different software becomes difficult, if not impossible.

Considering the stakes involved, software buyers do surprisingly little research themselves when making the decision as to which software to purchase. Instead, companies reach out to both consulting companies and IT analyst firms. Due to the lack of resources available internally to perform this research, most information about products to purchase comes from third party entities. As my book *Enterprise Software Selection* describes, it is very difficult to obtain objective advice on enterprise software because most of the entities providing advice on this topic have conflicts of interests. The poor quality of this advice is well known among those that work in the industry, but for whatever reason the lack of quality or objectivity is not generally stated in a published form.

Information technology analyst firms primarily sell their knowledge of software, hardware and services to those companies that purchase any of these items. They secondarily sell information related to vendors as well as information about clients to vendors. Information technology analyst firms—Gartner chiefly among them—are major influencers, not only on the demand side (that is, with companies that make enterprise software purchasing decisions) but also on the supply side (the software vendors themselves), as meeting the criteria of analysts can influence everything from the strategy that software vendors follow to their ability to raise money. However, while many opinions about analysts are available on the Internet, there are few authoritative sources about how analyst firms work and how to get the most out of them—for the demand side as well as the supply side, or for the investors. In fact, when doing research for this book, I checked the types of questions companies asked about Gartner. It seems that companies ask many questions about even the most elementary topics, such as what a Gartner subscription costs. Some IT analyst firms have a more straightforward offering—selling research reports for a specific published price, and in most cases they also offer consulting. However, because of the breadth of Gartner's offerings and how they control the information about these offerings and what they cost, understanding how to best use Gartner can be a challenge. This book combines answers to many basic questions in one place, but also provides the most sophisticated analysis to-date on everything from how Gartner performs research, to their internal incentives, their history, how to best deal with them, and most importantly how to interpret their research. This book aims to be the authoritative source on Gartner. The book will help readers understand what "lens" a Gartner research report should be read through, to understand why and how Gartner reports must be adjusted in order to understand them, and when it's more appropriate to contact Gartner with questions.

I have attempted to answer as many questions as possible in this book, and to get to the heart of what people generally want to know about Gartner. However, if you have other questions please leave them on the website for the book. I can answer your questions right online, and the questions may prompt me to perform further research and add sections to future editions of this book.

http://www.scmfocus.com/scmfocuspress/it-decision-making-books/gartner-and-the-magic-quadrant/

If you have any questions or comments on the book, please e-mail me at shaun-snapp@scmfocus.com.

Books on Gartner and IT Analysts
Before writing this book, I performed a literature review and found that there were no books on the general topic of IT analyst firms. I thought this of interest considering that the IT analyst market is close to four billion dollars per year. There were however, two books on Gartner. One book called, *Mastering the Hype Cycle: How to Choose the Right Innovation at the Right Time,* explains an analytical product offered by Gartner (I also discuss the product in this book). The other book is, *Up and to the Right: Strategy and Tactics of Analyst Influence,* which is written to educate software vendors on how to improve their ranking with Gartner. Current or former employees of Gartner wrote both books. When reviewing the paucity of literature on Gartner, I felt the time was right for a comprehensive and independent book that explained how to get the most from Gartner. In my viewpoint, too many people are using Gartner's research without understanding enough about how Gartner works.

My Background and the Book's Focus and Scope

It's important to cover my background so readers can understand my orientation, including my possible biases. Do I work for Gartner? Do I work for one of Gartner's competitors? Do I have a relationship with Gartner that may motivate me to write in one particular way about the company and its research products? All of these are important questions, the answers to which will help readers understand the information I present in this book. A main premise of the book is that Gartner must be understood in terms of its incentives and institutional structure before its research can be properly interpreted. So before we start with Gartner, let's start with me.

I am an author and independent consultant and I have spent my career working in advanced supply chain planning software. My consulting work has provided me with exposure to not only supply chain software, but also to ERP software, reporting, middleware and infrastructure software. I have never worked for Gartner, have never interviewed for a position with them, and have no past or present affiliation with the company. Through the years I have met a few people from Gartner, have seen some Gartner presentations at conferences, and have spoken to several people at Gartner while researching this book. Some people have said that I have, on several occasions, been called an analyst myself because I maintain a well-known set of websites under the umbrella of the scmfocus.com URL. However, when I compare the writing at SCM Focus to Gartner, it's clear that Gartner is directed toward an executive audience, while SCM Focus is for software implementers. As I discuss in Chapter 5: "The Magic Quadrant," while I do have an interest in comparing software applications in my software category, Gartner's research is frequently *interpreted* to provide more application-specific analysis, but in fact Gartner's methodology takes into account far broader criteria than the application.

One disadvantage of having never worked for Gartner is that I have not seen how the "sausage is made." Instead the evidence that I provide for the analysis in this book is based upon the research output, interviewing people primarily on how they deal with Gartner, and through an analysis of Gartner's methodology and their data. In fact, how Gartner analysts come to their conclusions is well known, although prior to researching this book I was not aware of their main channels for obtaining their information. It turns out that analysts are quite public about how they spend their day and how they acquire the information that goes into their reports. An advantage of not having worked for Gartner is that I had no nondisclosure agreements to deal with, and no relationships that I had to worry about maintaining. Thus I was less invested in any one viewpoint and was in a good position to be objective. Furthermore, I started with no particular agenda when writing this book and went wherever the data led me. While I would like this book to have as broad a readership as possible, I have not altered the book's conclusions in any way in order to achieve that objective.

I was disappointed in some of the conclusions that came out of my research into Gartner, as the conclusions I drew resulted in a book that may be more controversial than would be optimal if I were only interested in maximizing book sales. I could have papered over these controversial points, but then the book would not be research-based. The researcher who wants to be popular and not make any waves is probably not the researcher you want to get your information from. I believe that only through a comprehensive and accurate knowledge of Gartner can one determine the best way to interact and use Gartner. Among people who work in the industry, Gartner is a controversial company and topic. My approach has been to provide as much evidence as possible so that readers can decide for themselves. This book does not simply take Gartner's statements or Gartner's information as provided by them, through their website and other sources, and assume that the information is true. I have spent many years analyzing the statements made by software vendors, and if I simply accepted their statements at face value, my analysis would be worth very little. This book is an exercise in critical thinking, attempting to triangulate with multiple information sources and applying my experience in the field in order to come to a likely and plausible conclusion.

Gartner is an entity that can be analyzed from many different angles, including influencer, media outlet, research entity, social networking company, and several other roles. One's understanding of Gartner can be greatly enhanced by observing it through these different lenses. In addition, I have included quotations from professionals other than myself so that multiple viewpoints are represented in this book and different perspectives are provided.

It was a challenge to meet the needs of readers who work in many different capacities. As I know many people who work in a variety of functions in the enterprise software industry, I found myself continually asking myself what type of information a person who worked in this or that capacity would be interested in knowing about Gartner. There are many questions that buyers, vendors and investors have regarding Gartner. Gartner charges a high price for almost everything they do, so costs are an important topic. Furthermore, Gartner offers a variety of purchasing options for all of its customers and knowing where the "sweet spot" is in terms of how much to buy is valuable information. This book also talks about what benefits can be expected and for what cost, which will be useful when engaging Gartner. These costs—as well as the benefits—are not known perfectly and in some cases depend upon the company in question. I address these distinctions between customers in the different categories.

A second area addressed by the book is the methodologies used by Gartner. Gartner's results cannot be understood without understanding their various methodologies, and as soon as one does understand the methodology, the interpretation of Gartner's results completely changes. Through interviews with a number of people I have confirmed that most are not familiar with Gartner's methodologies used for even the best-known of Gartner's analytical products. In Chapter 9: "Is Gartner Worth the Investment?" I will propose what the company should take into consideration when using Gartner's analytical products.

Gartner presents potential customers with a wide array of offerings. This book does not attempt to cover everything that Gartner offers comprehensively because some of their offerings are really not that popular and are not what makes Gartner relevant. One should not simply read the Gartner website or even the Gartner annual report and take what they say they offer at face value. In actuality, Gartner is quite concentrated on a limited set of offerings, all of them based in some way on their dominant position in software vendor ratings (and to a lesser degree hardware and services vendor ratings). This dominant position in vendor ratings also draws in subscribers for other types of analysis such as articles on trends, mergers and general happenings in an area. This book focuses on the most well-known and commonly-purchased of Gartner's offerings, with the best-known of these being the Magic Quadrant. This analytical product is so central to Gartner that it has its own chapter.

The SCM Focus Site

As I am also the author of the SCM Focus site, ***http://www.scmfocus.com.*** The site and the book share a number of concepts and graphics. Furthermore, this book contains many links to articles on the site, which provide more detail on specific subjects.

Abbreviations

A listing of all abbreviations used throughout the book is provided at the end of the book.

CHAPTER 2

An Overview of Gartner

According to Wikipedia, there are over seven hundred and forty industry analyst firms globally. Of course only a fraction of these are IT analyst firms. Within the IT analyst segment Gartner is so dominant that it receives more than forty percent of all IT analyst firm revenues. Gideon Gartner founded Gartner in 1979, along with his partner David Stein. Prior to founding Gartner, Gideon had experience in IT as well as securities analysis. Gideon Gartner went on to found other technology research companies, including Soundview Technology Group and Giga Information Group. Gideon severed ties with Gartner back in 1993, when it had sales of roughly $120 million—Gartner has grown a great deal since Gideon's departure. Gartner's growth was not simply holistic; from the mid-1990s onward, Gartner consistently acquired up-and-coming IT analyst firms that were its main competitors. While Gartner began in the US market, its acquisitions are what allowed it to become a firm with global reach. During the late 1990s Gartner became an international IT analyst firm through its acquisition of companies like the French firm Abigail Engelsman, and the Singapore firm Datapro Information Services, Inc.

Gartner is one of the top mega IT analyst firms in the world. The IT analyst firm IDC (International Data Corporation) is close in terms of influence, but generally lower although still influential in different areas than Gartner. Forrester Research is the third mega IT analyst firm, but is roughly twenty percent the size of Gartner. While often compared directly with one another, these three firms **do not entirely overlap** in their offerings. For instance, IDC is more of a media conglomerate. Like Gartner, IDC sells research, but it is also a publisher of technology magazines. Forrester is known more for projection than vendor comparisons. At one time Forrester was close to Gartner in terms of their influence, but Gartner has now pulled ahead and is far more frequently quoted than Forrester (which of course is expected as they are more than five times as large as Forrester). Finally, Gartner has the broadest offering of the three companies, is the most global, and is the most influential in software selection.

Why Gartner Is So Important

Gartner was not always as influential as it is currently; its increased influence is due in part to its effectiveness in managing its business, and because it has gobbled up many of the other competing options. It has acquired more than thirty firms and it seems likely that Gartner will continue to acquire new firms in the future. New IT analyst companies are certainly free to try to fill the gaps left by these acquisitions, but it's not as easy as it sounds. It takes time for an IT analyst firm to develop its distinctive voice and build its prominence in the software categories that it covers. If one firm does rise in prominence, Gartner's financial position is such that they can acquire them as well with relative ease. William Hopkins explains this very well in an analysis of the Gartner acquisition of AMR Research.

> *"This may be the best acquisition ever—it kills two birds with one stone. Besides being a near perfect take-out play, it also offers easy access to a buyer base that is complimentary to their existing enterprise apps business. The best of both worlds. Here is why: The take-out play—As we have said many times before, one of the great ignored truths of the analyst space is how long it takes to build a buyer facing brand, products and sales force. Just like its acquisition of Meta, by buying AMR, Gartner removes the largest and one of the few remaining buyer-facing*

firms in the market. Our estimate is that it takes 12–15 years and at least $250 million dollars to build a buyer-facing firm."[1]

Something that Gartner itself certainly realizes is that there are significant benefits to being the biggest IT analyst in the market, including very strong competitive advantages.

Gartner's issuance of a report really means something significant to corporate buyers, and has real financial consequences for those vendors mentioned in the report, both good and bad. Gartner is in the catbird seat desired by many companies in that they are able to charge for information that many of the vendors pay to give them. Gartner is paid while it both gathers information and provides advice. Gartner is so influential that they control (in part) the fates of software vendors and set specific standards to which software vendors must adhere. Gartner has a series of preferences to which vendors either adhere or pay a penalty in the marketplace. As will be discussed at length, Gartner prefers its vendors to be big, and the smaller the vendor, the more of a disadvantage they have in scoring well. Other preferences will be described later in this book.

Not only is Gartner a major influencer in software purchases and vendor strategy, but less frequently discussed but also quite important is its influence on the stock prices of the public software vendors, and the ability of software vendors to raise capital.

Many banks and investment banks maintain subscriptions to Gartner and rely heavily upon Gartner's analysis to make their investment decisions. Investors don't even have the luxury of implementing software; so much of their information about software comes from sources like Gartner. The extent to which Gartner caters to the investor market is greatly underestimated by those who work in the software industry. This is covered in detail in Chapter 5: "The Magic Quadrant." Gartner is also hired by vendors to raise capital from investors.

---

[1] "Buyer facing" means that the company primarily provides research for buyers. Gartner is, in fact, both buyer and seller facing, but more of its income comes from buyers.

Gartner's Size and Scope

In 2012, Gartner had revenues of $1.615 billion with around five thousand five hundred employees. The best estimates I could find indicate that there are roughly nine hundred analysts and six hundred consultants, although sometimes the consultants are lumped in with the analysts, even though they have different jobs.[2] Gartner is headquartered in Stamford, Connecticut. As of this book's publication, Gartner covers thirty different technology areas, with many full-time analysts who focus on each of these areas. These thirty areas are listed below:

- Application Development
- Application Integration
- Business Process Management
- Business Process Platforms
- Collaboration
- Consulting and Systems Integration
- Content Management and E-Learning
- Customer Relationship Management Vision
- Data Management and E-Learning
- Data Management and Integration
- Emerging Markets
- Emerging Trends and Technology
- Enterprise Operations
- Environmentally Sustainable IT
- Enterprise Resource Planning/Supply Chain Management
- High Performance Workplace

---

[2] However, there are great discrepancies in how prolific and well-known these analysts are. A small percentage of the analysts listed above are responsible for a disproportionate amount of the research that is performed at Gartner.

- Innovation

- IT Sourcing

- IT Performance and Business Values

- IT Service and Enterprise Management

- Mobile and Wireless

- Open Source Software

- People, Work, Culture and Society

- Personal and Distributed Technologies

- Portals

- Project Portfolio Management

- Security, Profile and Risk

- Software as a Service

- Virtualization

- Web Technologies

The Gartner Business Model

In their 2012 annual report, Gartner makes the following statement about how they earn revenue.

1. Research: *"Gartner delivers independent, objective IT research and insight primarily through a subscription-based, digital media service. Gartner Research is the fundamental building block for all Gartner services and covers all technology-related markets, topics and industries, as well as supply chain topics. Our proprietary research content, presented in the form of reports, briefings, updates and related tools, is delivered directly to the client's desktop via our website and/or product-specific portals. Clients normally sign subscription contracts that provide access to our research content for individual users over a defined period of time, which is typically one year."*

2. Consulting: *"Gartner Consulting deepens relationships with our Research clients by extending the reach of our research through custom consulting engagements. Gartner Consulting brings together our unique research insight, benchmarking data, problem-solving methodologies and hands-on experience to improve the return on a client's IT investment."* According to their annual report, Gartner receives about twenty percent of their overall revenue from consulting.

3. Events: *"Gartner Symposium/IT expo events and Gartner Summit events are gatherings of technology's most senior IT professionals, business strategists and practitioners. Gartner Events offers current, relevant and actionable technology sessions led by Gartner analysts to clients and non-clients."*

Gartner's Network Effect

With Gartner's size, the number of areas covered, and the number of analysts that it can bring to these different topic areas, it is easy to see why Gartner is the largest organization in the world dedicated to the analysis of software. This type of scale provides significant advantages, including a large customer base that allows for a high number of return surveys, even if the percentage of participation is not very high on any one survey. This gets to an important point: a significant portion of Gartner's competitive position is based upon its interaction with a very large network of software vendors and buyers. The network results in a large database of individuals to which Gartner analysts can reach out when they are researching topics. This database—as well as the relationships that are developed through constant interaction with the people that make up this database—is by itself a significant percentage of Gartner's value as a company. Referred to as a "network economy of scale" or "network effect," an example is explained in the Wikipedia quote below:

> *"Many web sites also feature a network effect. One example is web marketplaces and exchanges, in that the value of the marketplace to a new user is proportional to the number of other users in the market. For example, eBay would not be a particularly useful site if auctions were not competitive. However, as the number of users grows on eBay, auctions grow more competitive, pushing up the prices of bids on items."*

That is, the more people and companies Gartner is in contact with, the more valuable is Gartner. If Gartner analysts did nothing more than stay in contact with this database of individuals to discuss various topics, they would know quite a bit. Analysts do not actually spend their time testing software, but tend to gain their information by reading, having phone conversations with buyers and vendors, and sometimes visiting sites. Gartner is also a frequent presenter at a variety of conferences and puts on its own events, allowing them to rub shoulders with a wide variety of senior IT professionals as well as bring together groups of buyers and vendors in customized sessions.

Gartner can be viewed as a social network, but one which is private rather than public (like a country club or a prestigious university where membership is expensive). People that read this might say "Wait, Gartner is nothing like Facebook." However, when I say a social network, I am not referring to the technology of a social networking site. Instead, I am referring to the theory of social networking, which goes back to the 1930s, and possibly earlier.

Gartner's Value As a Social Network

Gartner is a social network, while Facebook is both a social networking website and a social network. Facebook is so successful because it has managed to tap into the powerful desire of people to associate in a social network. However, social networks exist both online and offline. While Gartner distributes its research online, its social network is a decidedly offline affair. In fact, the information contained in Gartner's published findings is just the tip of the Gartner iceberg. Gartner is often interpreted as a research and consulting entity, but this misses a powerful part of their value-add.[3] (In fact, as we will see, Gartner is the strangest type of research entity.) And this value-add, while clearly understood by some, has not been explained in published form; interestingly, I was unable to find any published material on the topic of Gartner, or IT analysts, or industry analysts themselves as social networks. It seems that this observation has been missed by most.

---

[3] One reason that this is the case is that Gartner is not generally recognized as a social networking company. This is a textbook case of accepting what a company says it is rather than analyzing what it actually is.

SOCIAL NETWORK
ANALYSIS JOHN SCOTT

THIRD EDITION

Books like this one explain how to study social networks. Social networks were a field of study in academics long before they burst onto the scene with the creation of social networking sites.

In order to understand this aspect of Gartner, it makes sense to review the social network function and who benefits the most from a social network. Wikipedia's entry on social networks is a synopsis of the academic work in this area.

"In the context of networks, social capital exists where people have an **advantage because of their location in a network**. *Contacts in a network provide information, opportunities and perspectives that can be beneficial to the central player in the network.*

Networks rich in structural holes are a form of social capital in that they offer information benefits. The **main player in a network that bridges structural holes is able to access information from diverse sources and clusters.***"*

Gartner gains a great deal of power and authority from being at the center of the enterprise software social network. Gartner's research has authority not necessarily because it is right, or because there is any evidence that Gartner is able to select vendors that are the best fit for their subscribers (this would be hard to prove) but because it is popular.[4] Very few of Gartner's target market are researchers. They generally don't go back and read through old Gartner research reports to test for accuracy, but what they do know is that Gartner is read and respected by their peers and their superiors. Of course, the major characteristic of a social network is that its members value the opinion of their peers in the social network; their fellow members are heavy influences on any decisions they make. Therefore, if members of Gartner's social network read and respect Gartner's reports, that means a lot to the members of this social network.

The function that Gartner—or any information broker for that matter—can add through its central position in a social network is explained with the following graphics.

---

[4] While I believe a positive relationship must exist between Gartner's ratings and investment returns, I was unable to find any research to this effect. However, I am confident that an investment bank (or multiple investment banks) has performed such a study, although there would be no advantage to publishing such a study as it would make more sense to use the study results to make investment decisions. This is discussed in more detail in Chapter 9: "Is Gartner Worth the Investment?"

Social Network

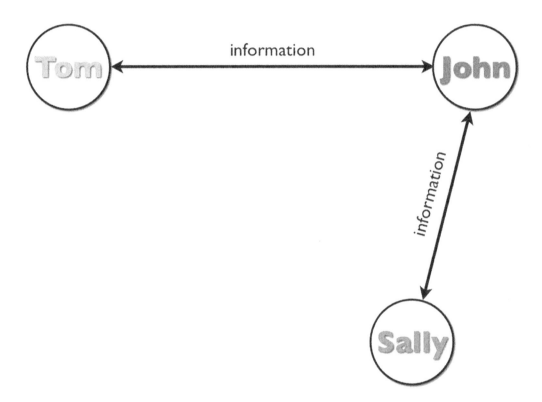

This simplified example represents the social network of three people with respect to IT information. (A person can be part of multiple social networks. For instance, each person has a social network of family, a social network of friends, etc. However, in this case we are filtering each person's social network for IT information exclusively.) Tom, John and Sally work with and have an interest in the same category of software. Tom and John work in different companies and share information with one another about their experiences. The same is true of John and Sally. John has two people in his IT social network, while Tom and Sally only have one person in their social network. Sally and Tom do not communicate with one another. Sally and Tom get some information that is passed to John, but not all the information.

Social Network

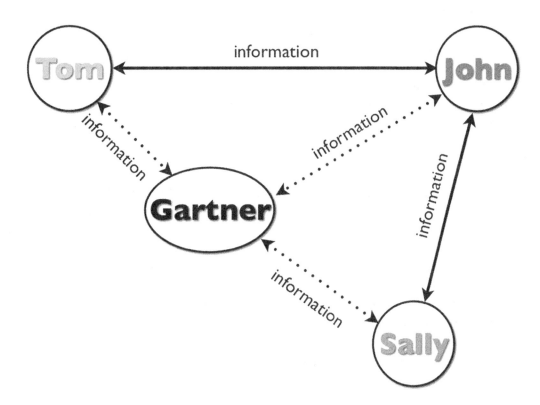

All three people do subscribe to Gartner, and Gartner fills in the gaps between Tom and Sally. Of course, Gartner also interacts with many thousands of other people in vendors, buyers, consulting companies, etc. Therefore Gartner is capable of filling "structural holes" between individuals.

Social networking sites are the common frame of reference for most readers, so it is interesting to see how Gartner is distinct from Facebook.

1. Gartner creates research products, which is a form of broadcasting, but also has one-on-one interactions—a form of "narrowcasting."

2. On Facebook, individuals are allowed to freely associate as long as they are part of one another's social network. Gartner, on the other hand, behaves more as a central hub, controlling the interaction. Except for events, where it, in part, charges for the right to connect up sub segments of the Gartner social network for freeform communication, the primary information flow is narrowcasting between Gartner and clients, and then broadcasting more limited and obscured information through research reports.[5]

3. Facebook monetizes its social network through both advertising and selling personal information about its social network members to various interested parties, while Gartner monetizes its social network with subscriptions, consulting services and events. Facebook does not interview or interact with its members.

4. Facebook creates a collaborative environment and allows the social network to self-organize, along with automated guidance routines that encourage members to enlarge their social network and become more involved with Facebook.

5. Facebook is a pure social networking site, while Gartner is a mixture of a social networking company combined with a research company, consulting company and information broker.

Generally Gartner is identified as exclusively a research and consulting company, but, in fact, it is much more than a research company. Its method of absorbing and providing information makes Gartner the "center of attention." Gartner researchers/analysts do not simply read vendor marketing literature, test software, analyze historical databases, and then release reports that can be purchased online. Instead their job is intensely social and much of their work and the work of other people at Gartner is about maintaining and nurturing that social network. One

---

[5] Gartner follows an "old school" approach to broadcasting. Since the development of blogging and commenting software, the predominant approach of articles has been to allow commenting, which adds significant value in many cases because readers can have perspectives and information that adds value to other readers. However, Gartner's publications are downloadable articles, with no ability to add or read subscriber comments. This is referred to as social media. It is curious that a company that specializes in technology research should employ such an old design to distributing information. Much more of Gartner's broadcasting could be moved toward a more modern information-sharing model; however, Gartner has shown no interest in adjusting their broadcasting/publishing approach.

cannot understand Gartner by *only looking at its media product*, because that is only a part of what makes Gartner the force that it is today. I made this mistake when I read my first Gartner reports more than a decade ago. By simply reading the content, I could not see why they were so influential. I should point out that social networking is a feature of all industry analyst firms; however, Gartner is particularly connected and particularly good at leveraging the social network it has created. They have in essence taken it to the next level.

Gartner As a Political Shield

Gartner's prominence allows them to provide an extra service to decision makers in companies that make purchases; these buyers can point to a Gartner rating, in say, a Magic Quadrant, as a defense against an implementation that has gone poorly. The decision maker can say, "Look, we did our due diligence, we selected highly-rated software; if there is a problem with the software it must have occurred during the implementation." Then when it comes to the implementation, typically companies will choose from major brands in consulting (for which Gartner also has a Magic Quadrant), and this is a secondary line of defense for problematic implementations. The same argument is used here: "Look, we selected recommended software and chose a major consulting company. What else could we have done?" In actuality a lot more could have been done. Selecting software that scores well in Gartner's Magic Quadrant and combining that with a major consulting company guarantees nothing. In fact, at large companies this is the predominant approach for software and consulting selection projects, and the success rate of enterprise implementations continues to be low and the costs continue to be high. Therefore, it is strange that the same strategy could be used as a defense or shield against managing projects ineffectively, but that is the reality of politics in companies. A great deal of playing the game of executive politics is making sure that you are never blamed for anything, and this points to the extreme conformity that exists in corporations. As I describe in the book, *Enterprise Software Risk: Controlling the Main Risk Factors on IT Projects,* executives often make purchasing decisions that are incredibly risky and, in fact, have a poor risk reward ratio, in order to choose an application that appears to be low in risk because it is an offering from a software vendor with a major brand. Gartner is a primary contributor to a misrepresentation of project risk through the large brand bias contained within the methodology of their research.

Procurement Agency Issues

There is, of course, what is commonly known as an "agency issue" with all purchases. The buying company is what is commonly known as the "principle," while the individuals that are entrusted with the purchasing decision are the "agents." The company would prefer, of course, that the agents it entrusts buy the best software for its requirements. However, the agents want to do first what is best for them. For instance, agents want to first and foremost keep their jobs. Many of the sales activities and behaviors of software vendors are designed to exploit this "principle-agency" problem. The agent faces a conflict when placing their political capital behind an application that they believe is the best choice for the company, but which is not rated highly by Gartner or by other influencers. The agent or decision maker is better protected politically if they choose the conformance view.

Gartner's Elite Orientation

Gartner has an elite orientation and this is demonstrated in several ways. The more I analyzed Gartner and compared it to other IT analysts, the more this characteristic became apparent. I have listed some of the ways in which Gartner is elitist below:

1. Gartner's analysts deal with the most senior members of buyer and vendor companies.

2. Gartner shares very little of its research for free, even for promotional purposes. The one exception to this is their market updates and predictions, which are selectively released as press releases. Gartner is effective at preventing the free dissemination of its research. By comparison many companies, including many IT analyst firms, have a blog of some type, which distributes some free analysis. Gartner does not do this (see the example on page 24 from Gartner's website). Unless part of Gartner's research is republished through a partner, their work is tightly controlled. This subject is one of the most interesting parts of how Gartner operates and will be discussed in detail in several places in this book.

3. Many IT analysts sell research by the article. For instance, you can search through Forrester's website and if you find an article that you like, you can buy just that article. Gartner does not allow nonsubscribers to search through their research database or, in most cases, to buy single articles. Gartner's model is to sell subscriptions as a starter or an introduction to their analyst consulting services.

4. Gartner seems to have an unlimited number of levels of service that one can sign up for, each promising more access to analysts and to more inside information. This exclusivity seems to increase the perceived value of research in the eyes of some clients. Gartner is proficient at marketing its upgraded services. For instance, criticism on the part of clients regarding satisfaction with their current service is quickly deflected by Gartner; whatever the client is dissatisfied with or whatever the client seeks is simply offered at the next level in service. Gartner's employees must be trained in this response because I have heard it used as a reflexive defense against criticisms that have nothing at all to do with the level of services purchased from Gartner.

5. All of Gartner's research, consulting and events are expensive. This means that not only does one have to pay to participate with Gartner, but the price of admission is quite high.

6. Gartner's broadcasting approach does not allow for user commentary, which also means that subscribers cannot read what other subscribers are thinking about the research areas. Most articles published today on the web (and this is particularly true of technology articles) allow comments. However, the communication on Gartner's articles is a one-way affair.

7. Because much of Gartner's advice to clients is not in a published form, only those with the budgets get to learn what Gartner analysts "really think."

Getting to the topic of how Gartner controls the dissemination of its research, notice the screen shots of Gartner's web page from an Internet search on two-tiered ERP systems on the following page.

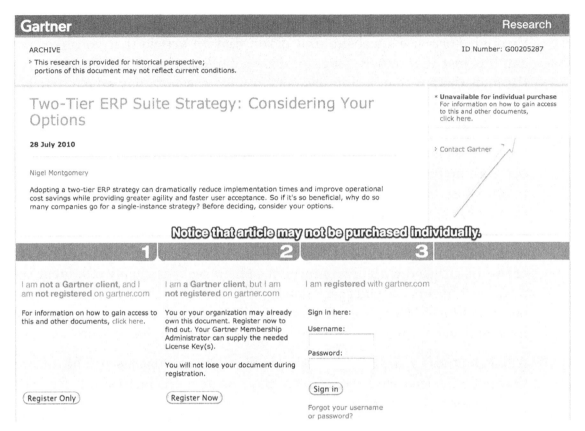

This result is a link from the Wikipedia entry on ERP systems. However, Gartner has only three lines of text that explain what the article contains. In the upper right hand corner of the web page it states that the article is not available for individual purchase, which means you must have a subscription—as with most of Gartner's research—in order to gain access to it.

TABLE OF CONTENTS

CONTENTS

Note at the bottom of the Table of Contents page is a listing that effectively tells the potential reader what they are missing.

Here is an example of research that can be purchased by the article.

Gartner's Sales Approach and Marketing Brilliance

Aggressive sales are a hallmark of how Gartner operates; they are aggressive in acquiring new clients as well as selling more to their current clients. A main complaint of Gartner's clients about the company is that this sales approach is too forceful, and employees who have left Gartner often leave because they cannot meet the high sales quotas that have been set before them. Those who have left Gartner and did not enjoy their time there will often describe Gartner as a "pure sales company." To thrive at Gartner as an analyst, one must be good at selling. While Gartner analysts do, of course, perform research, they are constantly selling their research and insights. Their sales goals became more challenging after the company went public, which I think must have had a negative effect on the research product. For instance, one reason why universities and very successful private research entities such as Bell Labs continue to have success is that they did not have such aggressive short-term pressure to sell. Most of the modern technologies that are the basis for our economy were developed not by corporations, with their short term profit goals, but by government research. This includes jet planes, semiconductors and the Internet. There would be few technology historians who would argue against the proposition that the two most innovative private research labs in the modern era were Bell Labs and Xerox PARC, two labs that were not coincidentally connected to AT&T and Xerox, companies with guaranteed year after year profits.[6] However, Gartner is a company that is continually pushing to grow.

I have analyzed a number of analyst firms and research organizations and I have never seen another company like Gartner that charges premium rates for what amounts to their marketing product, which is in some ways disguised as research output. As you read this book, regardless of the analysis I perform, understand that I consider Gartner to be brilliant from the perspective of marketing and in maintaining their negotiating leverage with companies. Any media company that seeks to charge a premium for its information can learn from Gartner. The fact is that few companies in any sector have accomplished what Gartner has done in these respects. We live in a period where journalism is in great decline because it is not able to get people to pay for news coverage. However, Gartner, a company that sells information—mostly about the enterprise software market—has never done better, and in most years continues to grow at a healthy rate.

The Nature of Gartner's Writing and Reports

All of the Gartner reports that I have read are well written, and much like *The Economist,* they keep a consistent tone and writing style despite the fact that a report could have been written by any one of Gartner's analysts. The way to

---

[6] Apple gets the credit, however, most of the early ideas that took hold in Apple, were not from Apple at all, but from Xerox PARC. Not only does this include the "idea" but in fact a working computer that was the Xerox Alto, which was introduced back in 1973. It was the first computer to have a graphical user interface, WYSIWYG printing email and a file server, a mouse, and was connected by Ethernet to a network, among a number of other innovations. The Alto was not commercially sold, but instead several thousand units were manufactured and used at PARC and other Xerox facilities and even at a few universities. Steve Jobs visited Xerox PARC in 1979 and was exposed to most of these innovations. These innovations that are ubiquitous today were developed out of the money from Xerox's monopoly profits on copier machines and related Xerox equipment. Interestingly, and something that is difficult to fathom from the modern perspective, while Xerox did a fantastic job innovating, they were not able to grasp the far ranging applications of their innovations. And it was not only Xerox, Steve Jobs took quite a few years to adopt the other Xerox innovations only taking the mouse and graphical user interface for the Lisa and Macintosh computers. The Computer History Museum in Mountain View, California has an Alto on display.

ensure this consistency is primarily to have good internal training for analysts and to make sure that a group of internal copyeditors go through all the reports written by the analysts. While the *writing* is consistent, reports from category to category and area to area vary a great deal in terms of their thoroughness and content. For instance, within the topic of Magic Quadrants, there is great variability in the amount of text dedicated to vendors based upon the particular Magic Quadrant in question. Secondly, some Magic Quadrant reports will quote survey results, while other Magic Quadrant reports will not.

Generally, Gartner reports are written for an executive audience. Most software-oriented people, either developers or implementers, are not the target audience even though the reports cover software in which these groups specialize. The people who spend the most time reading and discussing Gartner's research are:

1. Executives faced with purchasing decisions in companies that implement enterprise software

2. Marketing, sales and executives in the vendor companies

3. Investor analysts

Gartner's analytical products are unusual in that they use text to explain the research rather than graphics or numerical tables. Gartner tends to avoid using numerical tables—which would allow the user to see what Gartner is writing about in a comparative manner—and the raw data is rarely provided to the reader (something that will be covered in Chapter 4: "Comparing Gartner to *Consumer Reports,* the RAND Corporation, and Academic Research.") For instance, Gartner will say how a vendor performed in some survey area, but not declare how other vendors performed in that same survey area. This methodology is somewhat unique in this type of comparative research; in academic research or with *Consumer Reports,* tables are quite commonly used to compare all the data points—a generally-accepted practice that Gartner declines to follow. Gartner clearly prevents direct comparisons that normal publication guidelines for research would allow. And no wonder, as it is not in Gartner's best interests to declare its findings in black and white because those companies that it rates are also its customers. Therefore, Gartner's research feels more like a liberal arts paper than a research paper, as everything is interpreted for the reader rather than presented to the reader. As a consequence of verbose prose and the lack of anchoring comparative graphics, it is quite easy to get lost in a lengthy Gartner report, and it is quite natural for the reader to simply go back to the single comparison that is offered in the reports (for instance the Magic Quadrant graphic).

A clear political sensitivity comes across in the writing style used in Gartner reports and how information is disclosed to the reader. The writing approach also changes depending upon the type of report. For example, the writing for a Magic Quadrant document is dispassionate, while the writing for other articles (such as related to the future outcomes of mergers or technology market predictions) is more opinionated. Gartner also does a very good job of writing in such a way that rarely promotes one vendor over another. Occasionally I have come across Gartner research reports that are really just thinly-disguised press releases from a software vendor, but this is not representative of the vast majority of their research reports.

The transparency of the scoring of vendors depends upon the report category. For instance, in all of the Magic Quadrant reports I reviewed, I was never able to find one that actually showed the scores for the different criteria. Providing the criteria scores per vendor would be very useful, as the scores would allow buyers to adjust these reports to their needs and to better analyze the research. For example, if the actual scores per criteria were listed, buyers could alter the weighting of the criteria or eliminate the criteria that are not important to them altogether, which would be preferable over using the exact same criteria that are deemed relevant by Gartner. There are a couple of reasons as to why Gartner does not show the criteria scores. One: Gartner has to be careful what it writes in its most influential reports, because the vendors (which Gartner also counts as customers) review the analytical products as well. Two: the more oblique the reports, the more the customers must hire Gartner analysts for interpretation.

Alternatively, when the stakes are lower, such as in Gartner's *Top 25 Supply Chain Companies* report, a table with the criteria and the scores for each company is published. However, why is the difference so stark? This difference in the case of the *Top 25 Supply Chain Companies* (which coincidentally are not large buyers and customers of Gartner), those companies that do not find themselves on the

Top 25 list are not going to cut their subscriptions. With this less political report, Gartner is much more free to publish the scoring—and therefore they do.

Gartner's Varying Degrees of Disclosure

At other research entities, a standard of disclosure is applied for all research publications. Gartner's varying degrees of disclosure, which depend upon political considerations, would not be allowed at these other entities.

However, I do not want to give the impression that other research entities ignore political considerations when performing their research. More often than not, research from academics that is politically inconvenient is simply suppressed, or academic researchers self-censor and do not submit grants for certain types of research, or their research grants are rejected by the funding agency. Therefore, there are actually two issues:

1. *How much disclosure is there on published research?*

2. *How is politically sensitive research filtered out (i.e. not funded) before ever being researched?*[7]

In this case I am discussing the first issue and not the second. The footnote explains why an exploration of the second point is infeasible for this book.

---

[7] The issue of research suppression is hugely important. There are multiple cases of academic research being suppressed. Some research is kept private under false pretenses, such as for "national security" reasons. For example, RAND led the research project generally known as the "Pentagon Papers," which were not published because they contained the truth behind Vietnam. The papers were unknown outside of RAND and the Pentagon until they were leaked. The papers were kept secret not only from the public but from the President of the United States—who has the top security clearance and had every right to have access to them and be aware that a massive research project on the history of the US involvement in Vietnam was being undertaken. The reason for doing this was that if the President actually knew the real history of the US involvement in Vietnam, the Pentagon would be less able to control the interpretation of the conflict, of the US subterfuge of Vietnam and therefore less able to lead the President to the conclusions that the Pentagon wanted him lead toward.

Research suppression is more difficult to prove than differing disclosure standards between research. On the other side of the coin, a significant component of research has little to no benefit, as is pointed out by John P. A. Loannidis, a medical researcher who actually specializes in analyzing medical research. *"Many otherwise seemingly independent, university-based studies may be conducted for no other reason than to give physicians and researchers qualifications for promotion or tenure."* Research suppression is also a complicated topic, which is far beyond the scope of this book.

Gartner's Interpretation, Estimation and Presentation of Change

I reviewed many Gartner reports written over the years and with the benefit of 20/20 hindsight, I discovered some patterns. Gartner has what I call a "dynamic bias," which I define as the need to see things as much more interesting and innovative than they are in actuality. It was clear that Gartner has a tendency to overestimate the amount of change that occurs in any one software category, as well as the business developments in that category. Using the software areas in which I work as a sample, Gartner describes the business environment of this software as much more innovative and dynamic than it is in reality. This is interesting because Gartner developed a popular analytical product called the Hype Cycle (I cover the Hype Cycle in Chapter 6: "Other Analytical Products Offered by Gartner"), which is built on the premise that new technologies have an initial "Peak of Inflated Expectations Phase," often followed by a "Trough of Disillusionment." This is an acknowledgement by Gartner that it is much easier for a software vendor to simply develop a new innovative technology than it is for that technology to be implemented.

However, while the Hype Cycle clearly points this out (and is used by buyers to help them time their investments in software or other technology), I do not see it acknowledged in other Gartner writings. In fact, Gartner itself seems to drive hype cycles, which they in turn criticize in their Hype Cycle analytical product. This technique is used frequently by consulting companies to make their clients feel insecure about their level of progress. The more things are seen to change, the more demand there is for consulting and research services in order to keep up with that change.

Gartner's Large Vendor Orientation

In Chapter 5: "The Magic Quadrant," I demonstrate how Gartner's Magic Quadrant methodology clearly favors larger vendors. This over-emphasis on larger vendors is highlighted by many other people who have analyzed Gartner's reports. For example, Alan Pelz-Sharpe made the following comment when analyzing the Gartner report for his software category.

> *"There are other things about this report that baffle us—like why SAP is included in it, when even the report itself states that they do not have*

an ECM Suite—when others that do sell ECM Suites (such as those we mention above) are excluded. It may seem unfair to pick on another analyst firm—and for the record the authors of this particular report are all experts we have great respect for—but the importance of the MQ [Magic Quadrant] in the buying process is so huge that it demands a critical assessment and evaluation."

While this may be surprising to some, it is consistent with my experience with Gartner. Their Magic Quadrant is more about the vendor, and particularly the size of the vendor and how well it is established versus the application.

In defense of this approach, Gartner is not only explaining to its readers what currently is, but what will be. For instance, in 2002—prior to Microsoft having a business intelligence product—Gartner still stated with a ".7" probability that Microsoft would emerge as a market leader by 2005. This statement signaled to buyers that they may be able to get what they need from their preferred vendor if they postpone purchases of software for a few years. However, it also must be recognized that these predictions tend to be unique to situations where a larger vendor has some type of product limitation. I was not able to find a single instance of this type of statement made for a smaller vendor. A good indicator of bias is when a double standard like this is applied frequently. This is one example of large company bias, but there are others that I will discuss further on in this book. I will also cover bias in other analyst firms as well.

Gartner's IT Bias

Gartner tends to tailor its writing in a way that suits the interests of IT. For some time, IT's control of software selection decisions has been increasing. Gartner's growth has coincided with a reinforced influence of IT over software selection. This is demonstrated by Gartner's diminished focus on the application and amplified focus on things like integration, reducing the number of vendors from which purchases are made, etc. IT simply has different incentives than the business. When I discuss the inability of software (that the company has just purchased) to do the job, the business is all ears while IT does not want to hear about it. This point is brought out nicely in the following quote:

*"They think it's better to have fewer software contracts to manage
than it is to have the best technology for the business problems they
face. Companies should buy the best software for the job, not because
it's software from the vendor they already use. That's just plain lazy
and bad business."*—Christopher Koch, CIO Magazine

Estimating Bargaining Position

A valuable service that Gartner performs is estimating a vendor's bargaining
position. This of course is useful in helping a buyer during the negotiation stage,
and can help the buyer determine what type of offer a vendor may accept. This
estimation of bargaining position can apply to a particular vendor or to a category
of software, and can provide insight for a company that may want to invest in an
area. The following quotation from Gartner is fairly standard in this area.

*"'Up until now, the unique nature of the software market has meant
that buyers had very little negotiating power after the initial purchase
of a software license,' Gartner Vice President William Snyder said
in a research note. 'We expect those dynamics to change considerably
over the next 5 to 10 years, giving CIOs and software procurement
officers more bargaining power while potentially reducing software
vendor profit margins."*

*"Gartner also predicts that a fourth of all new business software will
be delivered by software as a service by 2011'."*

In fact, aside from broad-scale analysis of this nature regarding bargaining position, a Gartner analyst can advise companies on the relative bargaining positions
of different vendors from whom the buyer is interested in purchasing. In addition,
they also offer vendor negotiation services through their consulting arm.

A Touchstone of Perception

As I have alluded to previously, opinions on Gartner vary quite a bit among
people familiar with the company. However, regardless of one's personal opinion,
Gartner is generally recognized as influential. And its influence is greatest with
the people that have the most pull in the organization for enterprise software

selection. Gartner knows its market and what appeals to their customers very well. It designs its reports to be the type of report that will have the most influence with its client base.

Therefore, even a person who does not find Gartner's research personally useful can read a Gartner report and know what the perception of buyers is currently. This is how vendors use Gartner: simply to understand the competitive landscape. In this way, Gartner is a touchstone for perception for people from many different parts of the enterprise software world.

CHAPTER 3

How Gartner Makes Money

Understanding how Gartner makes its money is critical to understanding how it works and to interpreting the information they provide. As they say in political thrillers and investigative journalism: "Follow the money." This is important because it defines Gartner's incentives and operations.

According to their annual report, their 2012 revenue broke down in the following way.

Gartner's Sources of Revenue

Line of Business	Dollars	Percentage of Total
Research	$ 1,137,147.00	70%
Consulting	$ 304,893.00	19%
Events	$ 173,768.00	11%
Total	$ 1,615,808.00	
Net Income	$ 165,903.00	10%

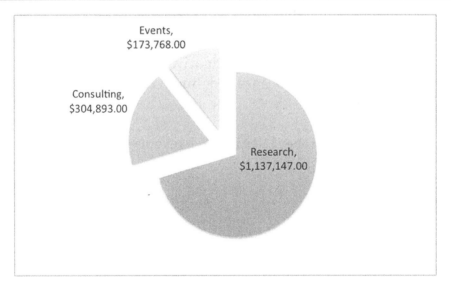

Gartner does not break out its revenue per line of business in terms of its customer category (i.e., buyer, vendor, investor, etc.), or its events revenue; however, Gartner receives revenue from buyers, vendors and investors in each line of business (research, consulting and events). Roughly seventy percent of their revenue comes from research-related activities and thirty percent from consulting and events. Actually, Gartner receives revenues from other types of customer as well.

For instance, they receive subscription revenue from consulting companies as well as from several other customer categories. However, in this book I focus on buyers, vendors and investors because they are Gartner's major customer categories. Furthermore, the explanation from Gartner's annual report as to what constitutes research is not entirely clear; when a company pays to talk to a Gartner analyst, this goes into the research revenue bucket rather than the consulting revenue bucket. Therefore the description for research should actually include both the subscription business and the analyst consulting business. However, services such as vendor contract negotiations would fall under the consulting revenue bucket.

Gartner is sensitive about their consulting revenue from vendors because at one point Gartner offered software selection services to buyers. Apparently this upset the vendors because the vendors were sharing information with the buyers that the vendors had obviously shared with Gartner in the first place. Gartner lost vendor consulting business, and thus made a conscious decision to reduce the depth of software selection services it offered. Gartner receives money from vendors through subscriptions, consulting and events. (Gartner charges vendors for booths and for access to buyers. For instance, in addition to putting on the conference, Gartner will do things like arrange special meetings on certain topics that are attended by a number of customers and one vendor.) The vendor payments reside in the roughly thirty percent of the business that is represented by consulting and events. Gartner says that their ratings have nothing to do with what services various vendors purchase from them. Gartner does not disclose which vendors pay Gartner or how much they pay. In fact, on Gartner's website there is no mention of the fact that vendors are also customers. The fact that Gartner is paid by the entities that it rates is brought up by people who know this fact, but Gartner makes every effort to keep this secret.

Gartner is by no means alone in this approach. In fact, it is the rare IT analyst firm that ***does not sell services to both buyers and sellers***. By having so much contact with buyers, Gartner develops databases of information that are of value to vendors, and of course vice versa. Gartner has created a number of consulting services that leverage the information that they accumulate through their interactions and research.

This is different from financial analysts who are often what is called either "buy side" or "sell side." Gartner provides both buy side and sell side analysis. This is the most common approach for IT analyst firms, but a few do diverge from this configuration. One example of an IT analyst firm that is only "buy side" is The Real Story Group. However, it is not a simple matter to find an exclusively "buy side" analyst for the software category in which you have an interest. For instance, I was unable to find a well-known IT analyst firm that did not sell consulting services to software vendors in my software category.

Public and Informed Opinion of Gartner's Payment Relationship with Vendors

The proposal that vendors need to spend money to improve their position with Gartner is openly discussed in the vendor community. This system is commonly referred to as "pay to play" and the term is extremely well-known in the industry. I named this heading "public and informed," because it is unclear how many people who read Gartner's research even know that vendors pay Gartner. However, the more people know Gartner, the more they are aware of this activity. I was personally unaware that Gartner received payments from vendors until the head of marketing for a software vendor explained to me how the system worked.

Gartner often sells what it refers to as technology advisory services, a few of which appear in a Gartner document on the topic and are listed below:

1. *"Will this database platform deliver the performance our application requires?"*

2. *"Will my key OEM partner be acquired?"*

3. *"What are the biggest issues people in this market are dealing with?"*

For instance, Gartner is interested in keeping up on all the players in a software category that they cover through what is referred to as an analyst briefing. Vendors give presentations to Gartner on their product, company and strategy, usually through some type of web meeting, and Gartner simply listens. This is explained in the following quote from Gartner.

> *"During a vendor briefing, the flow of information predominates from the vendor to the analyst and is not interactive. Analysts may ask*

*questions of clarification during a briefing session, however analyst
feedback is not the focus and should not play a part or role during
any given vendor briefing session."*—Gartner Vendor Briefings

The reason Gartner does this is because feedback from Gartner is charged to
the vendor ***as a consulting service***. If Gartner did not do this, then vendors
would be asking for feedback from Gartner and thus getting a free service. I
know something about this because I have often been asked for feedback from
vendors about how their application compares to others in the market. Gartner
analysts are well-versed in the game; if a vendor asks for information during the
analyst briefing, the analyst will respond that this is just an analyst briefing, and
that providing feedback is not what Gartner is there for. However, if the vendor
is interested, they can purchase a technology advisor service. At this point the
Gartner analyst has a well-rehearsed pitch that explains how the service works,
how large Gartner is, how much information they have to provide, and how other
vendors have previously benefited from Gartner's technology advisor services.
However, without purchasing this service, the vendor can expect nothing back
from Gartner.

Gartner has managed an amazing feat in that when they ask for information from
a vendor, they don't pay for the privilege; however, when a vendor asks them for
information, they must pay Gartner. This free information that Gartner receives
from vendors is analyzed, packaged and then sold to buyers. So when Gartner
wants information, it pays nothing, but when others want information from
Gartner, they pay. Gartner is running an excellent and very disciplined system.

You can read all about Gartner's analyst briefings at their website link:

  http://www.gartner.com/it/about/vendor_briefings.jsp

Much in the same way that buying a preparation guide for the SAT will improve
one's SAT test results, the amount of consulting services that a software vendor
buys from Gartner allows the vendor to better understand the grading that will
be applied to them. The difference is that SAT preparation books are universally
available and cost roughly twenty dollars, while Gartner's consulting services

are of course expensive and incomparable to other types of consulting costs in the industry.

> *"When with a previous employer, in one MQ interview I did it was suggested by the Gartner analyst that we were 'not visionary enough' for that part of the quadrant. When I asked what was visionary I was told that to get that information we needed to be clients. So I concluded that you had to pay to know what was visionary and then rework that into your vision in a nice circular process. So I do not know what the cost is but it seems to me you need to be paying to play."*—Nick Turner

All of this leads to the topic of the Gartner ombudsman.

The Gartner Ombudsman

The area that Gartner most often refers to as their check on bias is the Office of the Ombudsman, which manages against conflicts of interest and ensures fairness. Before we get into what the Gartner ombudsman is, let's start by analyzing the terminology.

An "ombudsman" is normally appointed by a government body and provided with the independence to investigate rights violations. The term "ombudsman" is infrequently used in the modern business environment. An ombudsman is similar to an Inspector General, something that everyone has heard of with respect to the United Nations. The definition of the Inspector General from the UN website is informative:

> *"UNHCR's Geneva headquarters has three mandated functions: to assess the quality of UNHCR's management, including identifying measures to prevent mismanagement and waste of resources; to investigate allegations of misconduct by anyone working for the agency, including non-permanent staff; and to conduct inquiries into violent attacks on UNHCR staff and operations, as well as other types of incidents that could affect the reputation of the organization."*

Gartner describes their ombudsman as follows:

> *"The Gartner Office of the Ombudsman has been modeled after that of the news industry, in which the ombudsman takes action on issues of accuracy, fairness, tone and balance submitted by newspaper readers or radio listeners. As in the news industry, the Gartner ombudsman recommends approaches to address these issues via content or process updates.*
>
> *At Gartner, these issues may be raised by clients, non-clients or employees. We don't simply react to comments from these audiences—we invite these comments with a dedicated Web site and staff that address issues as they arise.*
>
> *Given the nature of the current environment, we have formalized and publicized our commitment to objectivity to benefit both our associates and our clients. The ombudsman simply makes more public the ethics and standards we established when we were founded in 1979 and which continue to evolve."*

Sounds good, doesn't it? But, the explanation must be examined within the context of how different Gartner is from most media outlets, in particular with the statement that...

> *"The Gartner Office of the Ombudsman has been modeled after that of the news industry...."*

While it may be true that the office was "modeled" on the news industry, the position of Gartner vis-à-vis news industry firms is completely different; news organizations do not see every entity about which they write an article as a potential customer. To see why this is the case, let's perform a thought experiment. Imagine that *Time Magazine* was receiving payments from many of the entities about which they wrote articles. Of course, in a way *Time Magazine* does accept payments as they accept advertising. But, not every entity that *Time* reports on is a potential revenue source. Over at Gartner, however, every entity they report on is either *a current or a potential revenue source*. In addition, how much an advertiser advertises in a media outlet is a matter of public record. One can easily tell by reviewing the magazine, newspaper, television channel or website and checking who has advertised; this is why we know the relationship between financial contributions and the effect on media output. However, which software vendors pay Gartner—and how much they pay Gartner—is not a matter of public record.

Now comes the interesting part of the thought experiment. Could *Time Magazine* assuage people's concerns about reporting bias by simply saying, "It's OK. We have an ombudsman"? I don't think it could. In fact, let's take the example of the Swedish press Ombudsman.

> *"Pressombudsmannen (or press Ombudsman) is a person whose role in the Swedish print media is to determine whether the actions of a newspaper are in line with good journalistic practice. Complaints regarding the practices of print media can be reported by the general public to the Pressombudsmannen who determines whether a complaint should be brought before the Swedish Press Council (PON). The PON can issue fines of up to SEK 2,000 and publish a rejecting opinion."*—Wikipedia

However, notice that the press Ombudsman can refer the matter to the Swedish Press Council and a fine can be issued. There is no possible referral to anyone outside of the Gartner system. In fact, the actual complaints are not published, nor are the rulings, and transparency of the Gartner ombudsman is nil. While Gartner states that they have a dedicated website, it is used primarily for public relations to tell people about the effectiveness of the Gartner ombudsman. There is no publishing of information regarding current complaints.

Secondly, what is really known about the ombudsman in terms of his or her impartiality? For instance, let's imagine that a large vendor has a complaint regarding the fairness of a rating, while a smaller software company that does not pay Gartner (or pays a much smaller amount) has the same complaint. Which complaint would be a higher priority for the ombudsman? Anyone can guess, but there is no way to know for sure. Research requires data points, and Gartner does not publish the complaints, nor does it show how the ombudsman ruled. In a court case brought against Gartner by ZL, which claimed that Gartner's Magic Quadrant was "...*misleading and favored large vendors*," Dennis Howlett, writing for *ZDNet*, had the following to say about the ombudsman.

> *"Gartner currently has an employee act as ombudsman to handle disagreements. The conflict of interest is self-evident in the way ZL's concerns were summarily dismissed with little supporting evidence. There is a crying need to establish an impartial ombudsman similar to those found in public media, in order to ensure purchasers that they are receiving impartial analysis."*

So ZL proposed in the action against Gartner that the Gartner ombudsman is simply fascia and does not meet the standards of ombudsman in other areas, particularly in print. In this regard, ZL must be considered to be correct. Gartner could do a number of things to improve the Office of the Ombudsman.

1. The Office of the Ombudsman could be placed outside of Gartner and funded by software buyers.

2. The Office of the Ombudsman could publish the complaints and the rulings on these complaints on a public website.

As a research organization, Gartner should understand that their statements regarding the impartiality of their "ombudsman" are insufficient, for the same reason that Gartner should not accept a vendor's statement that they have "the best software in the world" or that they have "one hundred percent customer satisfaction," without actually asking for evidence of these claims. If research were just repeating what entities said about themselves, it would not be called research.

The PR Function of the Ombudsman

Gartner's description of the ombudsman function focuses on how the ombudsman rules on fairness complaints that are made to Gartner. However, this leaves out the ombudsman's quite significant public relations function. For example, the ombudsman—currently Nancy Erksine—is active on Internet comment sites stating that Gartner's ratings are never for sale. She also comments on the ombudsman website, generally saying good things about Gartner and so on. The ombudsman website also informs visitors that Gartner analysts are not allowed to own stock or have other types of investments in vendors.

The statements made by the ombudsman are designed to counter arguments that are critical of Gartner's objectivity. The entirety of evidence presented by Gartner regarding its objectivity essentially comes down to the ombudsman's word that Gartner has a number of controls in place, and therefore its research can be trusted to be without inappropriate influences. These statements are not auditable except by looking at Gartner's media output and by interviewing a number of people at vendor and buyer organizations, much of which would contradict the statements made by the ombudsman.

Another problem with the ombudsman's statements is objectivity. An individual has objectivity when they can reasonably be expected to be indifferent as to which way the results swing. For example, salesmen cannot be said to be objective between the vendor for which they work and the vendors that are competition because they are paid to sell the products of one vendor. They could not hold the position that the software of competing vendors is superior and continue to be employed. The same is true for the Gartner ombudsman. If Nancy Erksine were to begin telling members of the media that Gartner's vendor ratings can be purchased or that Gartner analysts take positions in the stock of vendors prior to the publication of Magic Quadrants, how much longer would Nancy Erksine be the Gartner ombudsman or be employed at Gartner? Since the answer is "not long," it is clear that the Office of the Ombudsman is not objective. Being objective means that it is at least possible for you to hold the opposite view from that which you currently hold. Gartner has borrowed the name of "ombudsman" for their mediating position, but have not imbued the role with the required independence to meet the definition of the term as it is used, not only in the media but in other areas as well.

What the Ombudsman Means for Vendors
Vendors should view the Gartner ombudsman as principally a public relations mechanism to make buyers comfortable with Gartner's reports and advice. If a vendor does not rank as desired in a report, appealing to the ombudsman will do

little. All vendors want to be rated superior to other vendors regardless of whether there is any justification for a superior rating. Gartner analysts are constantly hearing from vendors about how they think they should be rated higher than they were in the last review, so after some point, analysts will tune these vendors out. To improve one's rating in the future, a far more effective use of time and energy would be to hire Gartner to better understand their ratings and then do what it takes to score higher in these ratings. I will cover the value that can generally be expected from Gartner for technology advisor services in Chapter 9: "Is Gartner Worth the Investment?"

Conclusion

Gartner sells information to both buyers, sellers and investors. Its lines of business are research, consulting and events. However, the description for research actually includes both the subscription business and the analyst consulting business. As with most IT analyst firms, Gartner sells to both buyers and sellers. It is well recognized and a frequently discussed topic among vendors that vendors must pay in order to expect better positions in Gartner's ratings. Gartner will also not provide feedback to a vendor if they do not hire them for technology advisement services, and vendors are expected to provide all information to Gartner—which Gartner resells, for free. Some of what Gartner is paid for is analysis and organization of data, but some of it also is simply serving as an information broker and since Gartner has the largest number of buyers and vendors as well as investors as customers, it has the largest information network in the enterprise software area. In order to manage perceived conflicts of interest, Gartner has created the Office of the Ombudsman, which is taken conceptually from similar roles in the media and in other organizations, but which does not follow the generally accepted rules that help promote impartiality and is a process whose mechanizations are entirely hidden from view. The Office of the Ombudsman's greatest role is to serve as a public relations vehicle for the role of the ombudsman itself and to provide the perception that those who believe they are treated unfairly have some type of recourse.

CHAPTER 4

Comparing Gartner to *Consumer Reports,* the RAND Corporation, and Academic Research

I decided to evaluate the research output of Gartner by comparing Gartner's rules and business practices to respected research rules. A comparison of the research approach used by Gartner to that used by other analyst firms may seem like the long way around to understanding Gartner's research output, but I believe this chapter will greatly improve one's understanding of Gartner's research. While I have heard various criticisms of Gartner, I have never seen Gartner compared against respected research entities on important criteria. That is what is accomplished in this chapter. At the end of the chapter I compare Gartner to each of the other entities *in an easy-to-review form*.

One of the comparisons made in this chapter is between Gartner and what is probably the best-known rating company in the world: *Consumer Reports*. The second comparison is with one of the most respected think tanks in the world—the RAND Corporation—which has established a reputation for impartiality and sometimes groundbreaking research going back six decades. The third comparison is not with a single entity, but between Gartner and the academic research system to which most research institutions in the US, Europe and Australia/New Zealand subscribe. This chapter is important as it sets the stage for later chapters. My research for this book highlighted to me that far too frequently, Gartner is discussed in isolation without the broader context of generally-accepted research practice.

Gartner Versus *Consumer Reports*

Gartner Versus *Consumer Reports* on Funding from Rated Entities

Consumer Reports is the most trusted consumer rating and product-testing agency in the US. *Consumer Reports* has been continually published since 1936. *Consumer Reports* has a very structured and well-designed set of rules that strictly limits the influence of those whose products and services are rated by them. *Consumer Reports* takes no advertising or other forms of payments from those it reviews; instead it is wholly supported by their subscribers and is the largest subscription supported website in the US.[8] Compare this to Gartner, which takes money from those companies that it rates, actively solicits more business from current vendors who are customers, and solicits vendors who are not customers with what is generally known as aggressive sales tactics that stop just short of promising better results in their ratings.

The fact that *Consumer Reports* takes no advertising or other monies from those that they rate is a critical point. Their policy is different from JD Power and Associates, which is another well-known rating company. JD Power and Associates not only charges the vendors they rate, but charges vendors to advertise the JD Power and Associates award that they "won." They rate the winners in a category, but do not provide a complete list of the contestants, which is clearly a nod to the vendors who did not perform well in that category. These factors, among a host of others, is why JD Power and Associates is not seen as a serious research entity,

---

[8] Gartner's sales group clearly implies to vendors that they will improve their rating if they purchase consulting services from Gartner; this fact has been independently verified in multiple interviews I have conducted with people who work in senior positions out of the marketing department at software vendors. My confidence in this statement is reinforced by the fact that the same phraseology used by Gartner was quoted to me by these individuals, and the fact that none of these individuals knew one another.

and their principle usage is not by consumers but instead as something that advertisers use in order to create the illusion of a good rating with consumers.

Gartner Versus *Consumer Reports* on Vendor Use of Ratings

Consumer Reports also has a noncommercial use policy, which means that companies that are rated well by *Consumer Reports* may not use the *Consumer Reports* rating in advertising or even on their website. Generally speaking, this is the opposite from IT analyst firms and also from Gartner. Gartner has some restrictions on how the ratings can be used, but the limitations are quite liberal. The last reference to the rules regarding how Gartner's ratings can be used can be found on the Office of the Ombudsman website.

http://blogs.gartner.com/ombudsman/2012/12/11/important-updates-to-gartner-external-use-policy/

Software vendors frequently publish their Gartner ratings (if they are good) on their websites, "tweet" them, and put them in press releases. So software vendors advertise their Magic Quadrant rating quite aggressively if they have done well.

At first it may not seem obvious why it should matter if those companies that are rated use the rating in their advertising. The reason relates to the perception of endorsement that is made by the inclusion of a rating in such an advertisement, as well as the strong tendency a vendor has in spinning the rating to their ultimate advantage. Essentially, once vendors begin using rating results in advertising, *Consumer Reports* can no longer control the presentation of its results. *Consumer Reports* explains their policy in the following way:

> "At Consumer Reports, *we believe that objective, impartial testing, reviews and ratings are critically important for consumers. That is why we have a strict 'No Commercial Use Policy' preventing the use of our name and information for any promotional or advertising purposes. The policy helps ensure we avoid even the appearance of endorsing a particular product or service for financial gain. The policy also guarantees that consumers have access to the full context of our information and are not hearing about our findings through the language of salesmanship."*

Gartner Versus *Consumer Reports* on Controlling for Sample Bias

Consumer Reports buys all of the products that they rate. This allows them to be confident that the products they rate are the same products consumers would receive. If *Consumer Reports* did not do this and instead accepted free samples, these samples would deviate from what was available to consumers, as the manufacturers would make sure that only the best was sent to be rated. Not only do IT analyst firms not buy the software they rate, they don't actually test the software they rate. Ratings come from discussions with the software vendor, reviewing demos and questionnaires filled out by buyers, evaluating the literature produced by the vendor, and talking to companies that have implemented the software.

Therefore, Gartner differs quite significantly from *Consumer Reports* in that they do not actually test the products they recommend, and when Gartner does see the product, it is through a demo presented by the vendor in an artificial environment. Gartner uses a script during these analyst briefings, which means that the vendor must show what Gartner has on its script and may not deviate from the script. This is done to provide a consistent rating methodology to each vendor, but it has a disadvantage in that it prevents the presentation of what could be interesting and useful functionality. A number of individuals who have participated in these analyst briefings have informed me through interviews that the demos are in fact lighter versions of customer demos, which are themselves light compared to a demo that would be presented to a software-oriented person such as myself.

Gartner Versus the RAND Corporation

Depending upon who you ask, RAND is either the world's pre-eminent think tank or one of the top think tanks. RAND was created more than sixty years ago, before think tanks had acquired their poor reputation. In effect RAND is a "real" think tank, following—and in many cases exceeding—academic research standards. Although they are highly productive, they employ only roughly 1,700 people. Upon occasion I have read RAND research and was most impressed with the quality of their work. They were in fact a major innovator in an area of software about which I have written a book *(Inventory Optimization and Multi Echelon Planning Software),* and their research was featured prominently in that book.

The RAND Corporation began its life primarily doing research for the Pentagon. Some of their best-known research has been in the area of war gaming and strategies, which ranged from Vietnam (and from where was leaked the infamous Pentagon Papers) to the US anti-Soviet nuclear missile strategy. However, in the past few decades they have diversified into a much broader research entity that performs research on everything from energy and the environment to health care. RAND also publishes an explanation of the standards they follow. I did not use all of the criteria published in this document because some of the criteria do not relate to Gartner; RAND serves a public service function, whereas Gartner does not. However, a number of RAND's standards were universally applicable and they are discussed and compared to Gartner's standards in the following paragraphs.

Gartner Versus RAND on Referencing Past Work
RAND communicates very clearly how its research is performed.

> *"Although internal discussions about research quality have always been an integral part of RAND culture, more than a decade ago, we decided to codify in writing the quality standards for all RAND research. We intend the written standards to serve both as a guide for those who conduct, manage, support, and evaluate the research activities at RAND and also as the set of principles by which our research units and programs shape their individual quality assurance processes."*

RAND's *Standards for High Quality Research and Analysis* publication makes the following statement regarding how its research references other work.

> *"A high-quality study cannot be done in intellectual isolation: It necessarily builds on and contributes to a body of research and analysis. The relationships between a given study and its predecessors should be rich and explicit. The study team's understanding of past research should be evident in many aspects of its work, from the way in which the problem is formulated and approached to the discussion of the findings and their implications. The team should take particular care to explain the ways in which its study agrees, disagrees, or otherwise differs importantly from previous studies. Failure to demonstrate an*

understanding of previous research lowers the perceived quality of a study, despite any other good characteristics it may possess."

Gartner's research is very much encapsulated, and is much like *Consumer Reports* in this regard. A Gartner analyst might say that of course they don't work in isolation; they talk to vendors and client executives every day. However, that is not the isolation to which this statement refers. This statement refers to **other research**; and is **unrelated to whether one accesses data sources**. I write this as explicitly as I can, knowing full well that if a Gartner analyst does comment on this criticism in some public forum, that they will bring up the fact that they are not isolated and therefore I am mistaken and don't understand how Gartner operates. However, I can only declare this several times and let the chips fall where they may.

As with Gartner, *Consumer Reports* does its own research and is not reliant upon outside sources when it comes to product testing. However, *Consumer Reports* also writes articles on subjects like health care, and in those articles, *Consumer Reports* frequently refers to other research. One of the problems that *Consumer Reports* would have in quoting other product research results is: Whom would they quote? Other consumer rating entities do not follow anything close to the bias-controlled and thorough testing approach of *Consumer Reports*.

Gartner Versus RAND on Transparency of Research Data

RAND's position on transparency of research data is taken from the same RAND publication as the previous quotation.

> *"Data and other information are key inputs to research and analysis. Data-generation methods and database fields should be clearly specified, and the data should be properly screened and manipulated. The research team should indicate limitations in the quality of available data. In addition, information presented as factual should be correct and verifiable."*

Gartner's data is oftentimes not verifiable, for the main reason that frequently the data is not published. However, to meet RAND's standards the data from research **must always be published.**

Gartner Versus RAND on the Use of Jargon

It was interesting to see RAND take this position on the use of jargon:

> *"Necessary technical terms should be defined and explained."*

Gartner tends to use jargon in its writing. I recall one report that stated that a vendor's application performed "stochastic optimization." I was curious as to how many people who read the report actually knew what the term "stochastic" meant! Gartner basically assumes that the readers know all the terms that they use, but I do not recall seeing definitions at the end of their research. Although, in this day of the Internet where terms can be easily searched, it is probably less of an issue than it was in the past.

Gartner Versus RAND on the use of Graphical Elements

RAND has this to say on the topic of graphical elements:

> *"To help explain complex and novel ideas, the documentation should augment textual exposition with graphical or pictorial elements."*

Gartner does not do this. I concluded some time ago that graphical elements were important to explaining complex information, but it was interesting to see RAND make it a priority.

Gartner Versus RAND on the Tone

This one seemed a little superficial at first glance, but upon reflection it makes sense why RAND lists a "temperate" tone as an objective of their research.

> *"High-quality research documentation should be temperate in tone. It should sound neither so flat as to appear unengaged nor so emotional as to appear partisan. Almost all RAND research is relevant to two intersecting sets of discussions: one among analysts, and another among decision makers. A temperate tone is best suited to both communities, as well as to wider audiences, such as the general public."*

Gartner certainly adopts a temperate tone in all of the reports that I read as research for this book. In fact, the tone was a clear characteristic that comes out immediately when reading a Gartner report.

Gartner Versus Academic Research Standards

Gartner Versus the Academy on Peer Review

Gartner's research is to a degree peer-reviewed prior to publication, but not with peers outside of Gartner. In academics, research is always peer reviewed outside of the institution. According to Wikipedia: *"Publications that have not undergone peer review are likely to be regarded with suspicion by scholars and professionals."*

A lack of peer review can come across as a researcher having a particular bias, or that a researcher was not confident that the findings could survive a peer review. One of the best examples of the mistakes that can occur when research is not peer-reviewed is the example of cold fusion. In 1989, Stanley Pons and Martin Fleischmann, along with the University of Utah, submitted a research paper to the journals *Nature* and *The Journal of Electroanalytical Chemistry*—at the same time that they released a press release saying that they had discovered a way to create a nuclear reaction at room temperature. Pons and Fleishmann predicted to members of the media that:

> *"...cold fusion would solve environmental problems, and would provide a limitless inexhaustible source of clean energy, using only seawater as fuel. They said the results had been confirmed dozens of times and they had no doubts about them."*

The world was on its way to clean and limitless energy. There was only one problem: the results recorded by Pons and Fleischmann could not be replicated by other research teams that followed their methodology. The results, which led to the cold fusion rush, were eventually chalked up to poor research controls and to the conclusion that Pons and Fleischmann had measured their study incorrectly. This research, which had not been peer-reviewed, led to a number of negative consequences including many millions of dollars spent in the subsequent decade—mostly by private industry—to replicate the faulty results. However, if Pons and Fleischmann and the University of Utah had followed the normal academic protocol of waiting to announce their results until after their experiment had been peer-reviewed and attempts had been made to replicate the results, the term "cold fusion" would not be in the popular consciousness because there would have been nothing to report.

The Issue Gartner Would Face if its Research Peer Reviewed
Peer review works in the academic system because these institutions are part of a large ecology of universities that have worked this way for quite some time and it is the accepted practice. It would be very difficult for Gartner to have its research peer-reviewed. Who would review it: Forrester? These entities are all for-profit companies that do not share information with other companies—a major limitation with research conducted by private entities. The research of *Consumer Reports* is not peer-reviewed; however the transparency with which it publishes its reports makes *Consumer Reports* auditable. The lack of peer review, along with an inability to audit Gartner's results, is a problematic combination, which will be explored in the conclusion of this chapter.

Gartner Versus the Academy on Publishing the Methodology
The methodology used for research is such an important part of the disclosure of scientific papers that it is part of the IMRAD acronym, which is commonly discussed in academics. This stands for:

1. Introduction

2. Methods

3. Results

4. (and)

5. Discussion

This is the normal order in which academic papers are presented.

Does Gartner Publish Its Methodology?

A number of headings on Gartner's website use the term "methodology." Some can be found below:

http://www.gartner.com/technology/supply-chain/top25_methodology.jsp

http://www.gartner.com/DisplayDocument?doc_cd=154752

These pages do provide information about the methodology, as does the research. Generally it is clear, at least to me, what each of Gartner's research reports is measuring. However, as a person who has read quite a bit of research, I would classify Gartner's disclosure on methodology as very light. Essentially Gartner is misleading many of its subscribers (who do not have a research background) into believing that this is a normal level of disclosure.

For instance, let's look at the methodology for the Magic Quadrant. The criteria used and which make up each axis are declared; however, are they all given equal weight or are some weighted more than others? What Gartner considers as disclosure of its methodology would not be considered a full disclosure by any of the research entities that I have discussed up to this point. In fact, Gartner's results, as published to subscribers, would never be published in any journal. Not all IT analysts follow this concealed approach. Forrester is one. Donald Ham explains how Forrester's Wave (a competitor to Gartner's Magic Quadrant) discloses much more to subscribers and allows subscribers to gain more value from the research.

> *"Forrester's Wave product, their graphical vendor comparison tool, is similar in approach to the well-known Gartner Magic Quadrant. However, the wave lets end users change relative weights of the comparison criteria by downloading and interacting with an Excel spreadsheet, resulting in a graphical display customized for the specific need—a very cool enhancement. Forrester is not as prolific with Wave reports as Gartner is with MQs, but where they exist for the products you're investigating, points go to Forrester."*

The following table shows the criteria, the weights, and the data from Forrester's Wave on BI Service Providers.

Figure 6 Forrester's Wave™: BI Services, Q4 '12 Strategy Evaluation (Cont.)

	Forrester's Weighting	Accenture	Capgemini	Cognizant	CSC	Deloitte	HP	IBM	Infosys	KPMG	PwC	TCS	Wipro
CURRENT OFFERING	50%	4.84	4.23	3.38	3.94	4.67	3.26	4.85	4.00	4.33	4.45	4.06	4.01
Competency	60%	4.97	4.03	3.35	3.53	4.73	3.34	4.99	3.71	4.57	4.57	3.50	3.66
Relationship	20%	4.45	4.93	4.45	4.35	4.38	3.89	4.38	5.00	3.93	4.45	4.90	4.90
Results	20%	4.85	4.15	2.40	4.78	4.78	2.38	4.93	3.85	4.03	4.13	4.93	4.20
STRATEGY	50%	4.90	3.70	3.95	4.55	4.55	4.55	5.00	3.95	4.20	3.35	3.35	3.95
Non-client-facing R&D resources	60%	5.00	3.00	4.00	5.00	5.00	5.00	5.00	4.00	5.00	3.00	3.00	4.00
Level of importance	0%	5.00	5.00	5.00	5.00	5.00	5.00	5.00	5.00	5.00	5.00	5.00	5.00
Scope of offerings	35%	5.00	5.00	4.00	4.00	4.00	4.00	5.00	4.00	3.00	4.00	4.00	4.00
BI market knowledge	0%	5.00	5.00	5.00	5.00	5.00	5.00	5.00	5.00	5.00	5.00	5.00	5.00
Use of BI methodology within one's business	5%	3.00	3.00	3.00	3.00	3.00	3.00	5.00	3.00	3.00	3.00	3.00	3.00
Knowledge of industry-vertical-specific business processes	0%	5.00	5.00	5.00	5.00	5.00	5.00	5.00	5.00	5.00	5.00	5.00	5.00
MARKET PRESENCE	0%	4.60	3.60	3.80	3.00	3.80	3.80	4.60	3.60	3.60	3.00	3.60	3.20
Firm revenues and FTEs	20%	3.00	3.00	3.00	3.00	3.00	5.00	5.00	3.00	3.00	3.00	3.00	3.00
BI revenues and FTEs	20%	5.00	3.00	4.00	2.00	4.00	3.00	5.00	3.00	3.00	3.00	5.00	3.00
BI customers and projects	20%	5.00	4.00	4.00	1.00	3.00	4.00	5.00	3.00	5.00	2.00	2.00	2.00
Global presence	20%	5.00	4.00	4.00	4.00	5.00	4.00	5.00	5.00	5.00	5.00	5.00	5.00
Alliances	20%	5.00	4.00	4.00	5.00	4.00	3.00	3.00	4.00	2.00	2.00	3.00	3.00

All scores are based on a scale of 0 (weak) to 5 (strong).

Source: Forrester Research, Inc.

A good example of a far more complete disclosure of the methodology is available at the website for statistics for the Netherlands. I have included this link so that readers can gain an understanding of what I am describing.

http://www.cbs.nl/en-GB/menu/methoden/default.htm

The following argument is used by ZL Tech's CEO Kon Leong, the company referred to previously that sued Gartner for damaging its business by unfairly ranking its products versus competitor's products because of the company's smaller size (its lawsuit was eventually rejected).

> *"The tech industry would benefit if Gartner were required to disclose more data in its evaluation process and disclose component scores, so vendors know exactly where they are lacking and by how much and take corrective action."*

It is important to consider that Gartner's target market is not researchers, but rather decision makers who are buyers, vendors and investors. Many (but not all) of the people in these groups will be more interested in simply seeing the results. In fact, there are many who question how many of the people who read and rely upon Gartner's reports **actually read the entire report,** much less understand the research methodology. This gets back to the main theme throughout this book—that Gartner's research is not particularly useful without the context provided by Gartner analysts. However, because the privately provided information is not part of the public record, it is also not auditable.

How the Methodology Is Interpreted

Methodology is one of the most overlooked areas of Gartner by those who read its research. The criteria are often not what one would expect to be used, and if you speak with most people about Gartner's methodology, it turns out they don't actually know the methodology. I can say this with confidence because when I tell interviewees what makes up the criteria for different analytical products, I frequently receive the response: "Is that what is counted by Gartner?"

Gartner itself has stated that readers are too quick to review a single graphic and not read the entire report. On the other hand, the way Gartner comments on its research is also responsible for providing the wrong impression regarding their methodologies as I will demonstrate. I explain this in Chapter 5: "The Magic Quadrant." However, for the sake of continuity let me provide another example: Gartner's "Supply Chain Top 25."

The Gartner Supply Chain Top 25

Gartner publishes a "Supply Chain Top 25," which most people would assume is the twenty-five companies that have the highest-performing supply chains (that is, the highest performance from the metrics normally associated with supply chain management—things like forecast accuracy, inventory turnover, service level, and other similar measures). However, upon reading Gartner's methodology for creating the Supply Chain Top 25, only one of these criterion are used. The criterions are instead:

1. *Return on Assets (ROA)—Net income / total assets*

2. *Inventory Turns—Cost of goods sold / inventory*

3. *Revenue Growth—Change in revenue from prior year*

4. *Gartner's Internal Voting*

5. *Gartner's Client's Voting*

Two of the criteria that determine the Supply Chain Top 25 do not have anything to do with supply chain at all, but have to do with financial performance! However, when I read Gartner's explanation of the research to media outlets, I found it did not match up with the methodology. The quotation below is an example of this.

> *"At the heart of the Supply Chain Top 25 is the notion of demand-driven leadership," said Debra Hofman, managing vice president at Gartner. "We've been researching and writing about demand-driven practices since 2003, highlighting the journey companies are taking: from the old 'push' model of supply chain to one that integrates demand, supply and product into a value network that orchestrates a profitable response to ever-shifting changes in demand."*

Debra Hofman's explanation is not the primary methodology of the study. Instead, the methodology focuses on the financial performance of the overall firm combined with people voting for who they thought should be on the list. As I've explained, the heart of the study is the methodology, not the notion of "demand-driven leadership." The only control over whether a company showed "demand-driven leadership" is the one criterion, which Gartner voted on. The other four criteria could not have been related to this.

Furthermore, the definition of "demand driven" is quite hazy. I work in the field, and am unsure as to whether I have heard the term used before. Furthermore, the term "demand driven" is not used a single time in the report itself. If it is such an important component to the report, why is it not part of the methodology and not part of the report?

Conclusion

In the tables below, I have organized the scores of Gartner and of each of the comparison entities. The tables have a few more criteria than included in this chapter. These criteria were excluded from the text to keep the chapter to a manageable length. The tables rank all entities against Gartner on every criterion:

Gartner Versus Consumer Reports, RAND and Academic Research: Descriptions

	Compared Entities			
Criteria	*Gartner*	*Consumer Reports*	*RAND*	*Academic Research*
Funding Reported from Rated or Researched Entities	No	N/A	Yes (Entity which sponsors is listed on the first page of the report), but specific quantities are not listed. They list all contibutors over $100,000	In most academic areas yes, but bio-medical research is an exception and there is little enforcement of conflicts of interest)
Research Entity Restricts the Vendor (or research subject) Use of Rating or Results	Some, but minor.	Yes, and CR forbids the use of its ratings by vendors.	This issue does not generally apply to RAND as the nature of the research is non-commerically related.	Mostly not an issue, again except in bio-medical research.
Controlling for Sample Bias (of tested items)	Not an issue with respect to product testing as Gartner is not a testing entity.	CR buys the products it tests without informing the vendor.	N/A	N/A
References Past Work in the Field	Gartner is self contained. All of its research is original and they do not refer other work.	When it comes to product testing CR does not refer to outside studies. However, other CR research such as articles on pharmaceuticals does reference research literature.	Yes	Yes

Gartner Versus Consumer Reports, RAND and Academic Research: Descriptions

Criteria	Compared Entities			
	Gartner	Consumer Reports	RAND	Academic Research
Transparency of Research Data	Generally not, and not on the most important research, but sometimes Gartner will include a table with the actual criteria scores.	Yes	Yes	Yes
Changing Degree of Disclosure of Research Results Depending Upon Political Considerations	Yes	No	No	No, but complete consistency cannot be enforced as easily as so many entities are involved.
Research not Left Out of the Publication or Subcription. No Review with Researcher/Analyst is Necessary	Yes	No	No	No
Use of Jargon	Yes	No	No	Yes. However, academic research is not generally designed to be read by non experts in the field.

Here you can see a description of how each entity performed in each criterion. Based upon this description I have assigned a score, which are shown on the following table:

Gartner Versus Consumer Reports, RAND and Academic Research: Descriptions

Criteria	Compared Entities			
	Gartner	Consumer Reports	RAND	Academic Research
Use of Graphic Elements	Few graphical elements aside from the singular graphic of the report such as the hype cycle or the magic quadrant.	Yes	Yes	It very much depends. No generalization can be made.
Temperate Tone	Yes	Yes	Yes	Yes
Peer Review	Internal peer review, but not External peer review.	Internal peer review, but not External peer review.	Partially, by one RAND staff member and one outside expert.	Yes
Publishing the Methodology	Yes, but less so than the three other entities.	Yes	Yes	Yes
Declaration of Conflicts of Interest	No	N/A (Consumer Reports policy is to not allow conflicts of interest to exist)	RAND has a conflict of interest by the fact that it accepts money from many companies, however it is not rating the entites. Still its research could benefit these entities if RAND's research results in policies that help these entities. RAND has a stringent conflicts of interest policy -- for its health research arm.	Yes, but enforcement of non-declaration has few penalties. Bio-medical research has major conflicts of interests, with research physicians receiving payments from pharmaceutical companies and medical equipment companies. Conflicts of interest keep growing as universities increasingly "partner" with industry.

1. The scoring methodology is that the higher the score the better. The entity receives a ten if the issue does not apply to them. For instance, *Consumer Reports* does not receive any funding, so the issue of reporting industry funding does not even come up.

2. The zero and ten scores were simple to score; however, when the criteria was not binary, the scoring required some judgment or subjectivity. Of the four entities, academic research was the most difficult to score because, while there are generally-accepted research principles, there is considerable variability in their adherence. Not only is there the issue of bio-medical

research, which operates quite differently from other types of academic research, but there is the issue of public versus private universities, among just a few of many variable factors.

3. Given RAND's excellent reputation for impartiality and transparency, I was surprised that I was not able to find any record of financial contributions, or even ranking of donors from large to small. In all the research entities that I studied, it is concerning that it is so difficult to determine exactly how much money is contributed by each entity. Although there is no question of which entity funds each of RAND's research reports and RAND lists its contributors (which is far more transparent than Gartner), this disclosure is still below what I would like to see. To see how transparent RAND is on this topic, I have included below an example of the statement incorporated on the front of each paper:

> *"This research is supported by the United States Air Force under Project RAND—Contract No. F44620-67-C-0045—monitored by the Directorate of Operational Requirements and Development Plans, Deputy Chief of Staff, Research and Development, Hq USAF. Views or conclusions contained in this study should not be interpreted as representing official opinion or policy of the United States Air Force."*—Descriptions of The Computer Program for Metric—A Multi-Echelon Technique for Recoverable Item Control

This makes it clear who funded the study, even if we are not told how much funding was received.

Academic research is far hazier in terms of listing contributors, as the university contributors are never actually listed on the reports. Instead the money tends to go into a big pot for each university department. But it would be difficult to doubt its corrupting influence. One of the more amusing contributions from industry was the $100 million that Exxon Mobile paid Stanford to fund climate and energy research. One can imagine what type of "research" Stanford will be doing with this money, and how many times this grant will be mentioned on Exxon Mobile marketing material.[9]

Because *Consumer Reports* is subscriber-supported, no one in the comparison group could match *Consumer Reports* in their lack of conflicts of interest. I did not weigh the criteria as I would normally do in a software selection matrix, but instead considered each criteria equal in weight. In my opinion, the criteria should not be equally weighted, but I wanted to keep the presentation of the table simple.

The Scores

The scores were quite interesting; as you can see from the table on page 62, Gartner scored quite low when compared to the other three research entities.

Reasons for Gartner's Low Score

Gartner lost points for a lack of transparency in several areas related to both data and conflicts of interest. I was hoping that at this point the reader would have figured out that this, in fact, is the type of report that Gartner would produce. Now, certainly Gartner analysts will not agree with the table and its findings. They may criticize individual criterion as not representative of good research practices (not a very good argument), but more likely, they will declare the entire exercise meaningless because Gartner cannot be compared to the other research

---

[9] One of the things that made US universities the respected research institutions that they were was that the public universities had a single contributor: the US government. The US government has a history of a long-term commitment to research without the necessity for a commercial outcome. Corporations cannot come close to matching this commitment. However, as the US university system increasingly is privately funded, conflicts of interest become more common. These quotations are from Cal State University website: *"At a recent debate before Stanford's Academic Senate, respected law professor Hank Greely argued that the tobacco industry 'has perverted academic research for its own ends in ways that have had horrific consequences.'*

'It hurts me that my university gives them cover and sustenance,' said Greely, a co-author of the resolution. 'They are using us to whitewash themselves.'

For decades, university-based research funding was a strategic element of the tobacco industry's effort to whitewash its tarnished public image.

Its disingenuous research was a focal point of a landmark trial last summer. On Aug. 17, 2006, Judge Gladys Kessler of the Federal District Court for the District of Columbia ruled that the tobacco industry had engaged in a 40-year conspiracy to defraud smokers about the health risks of tobacco. As evidence, she cited industry-sponsored work by UCLA epidemiologist James Enstrom, who challenged the view that second-hand smoke poses a serious health risk."

entities as they are so unique. (Actually, Gartner would not score very well against other IT analyst firms. They would lose points against, say, Forrester because Forrester discloses their research data.) At least these are the arguments that I would expect.

However, if we pause for a moment, it should be clear that what I have laid out in these tables has a number of advantages over the research presented by Gartner. Here is how my research differs from Gartner's:

1. I explained the methodology for how I would determine the description of each criteria per entity (this has been laid out in the comparison sections of this book).

2. The methodology of the scoring has been explained: it is based upon the descriptions.

3. The actual complete research data set was shown and anyone can see the scores for each criterion.

4. Although I have not yet made this declaration, it should be relatively obvious that I am not selling consulting services to *Consumer Reports*, RAND or the general academic community, and I have no conflict of interest that could pollute my results.

Therefore, while Gartner analysts may criticize the research at their leisure, the research adheres to a standard that no research produced by Gartner can claim to match.

Profit or Nonprofit and Why It Matters for Research Quality

A final point, and a criterion that I considered adding, is whether the research entity is nonprofit. For-profit entities have a harder time maintaining research integrity over nonprofit entities. This is a major reason as to why government-funded research out-performs private research. Private research has so many disadvantages, including the fact that it does not share its research results with the research community. If we take one of the most prolific private research entities that ever existed—Bell Labs, an entity responsible for a long laundry list of technologies ranging from the transistor to the laser and the winner of multiple

Nobel Prizes—it is recognized that their success was precisely because Bell Labs was funded by what amounted to a government granted/regulated monopoly in the form of Bell Telephone. When the government broke apart Bell Telephone's monopoly, the Bell Labs' ability to produce at the same level declined. Similar labs existed (although none as prominent as Bell Labs), such as RCA Labs and Xerox PARC. The relationship is clear: the more public in nature the entity, the better it can support research and maintain the integrity of its research. Of the research entities compared, only Gartner is for profit. The other three are nonprofit. Of course none of the other three entities is a viable option for a decision-maker to use as an IT analyst. IT analysts are all private for profit entities. Because of this, companies that seek to use the research output must be careful how they use the research output from these companies.

CHAPTER 5

The Magic Quadrant

The Magic Quadrant is a simple and well-known graphic, and is the best-known research produced by Gartner. The Magic Quadrant places a software vendor on a matrix, with completeness of vision on one axis and ability to execute on the other.

A frequent question people have about the Magic Quadrant is how many of these graphics Gartner produces. The full list of Magic Quadrants produced by Gartner can be found on Gartner's website at the link below.

http://www.gartner.com/technology/research/methodologies/
magicQuadrants.jsp

However, many of the Magic Quadrants produced by Gartner have been discontinued. Using Gartner's spreadsheet I found one hundred and twenty six magic quadrants. However, it's clear this spreadsheet is missing several entries, as I am aware of Magic Quadrants that are not on the list. Furthermore, there are several Magic Quadrants that I have from the mid 2000s that Gartner used to produce but does not list as retired Magic Quadrants.

An example of a Magic Quadrant is shown below:

According to Gartner *"Magic Quadrants depict markets in the middle phases of their lifecycle...."* Depending upon how the software vendor rates, they are placed into one of the following four quadrants. These quadrant descriptions are from Gartner's publication *Inside Gartner Research*.

1. Leaders: *"Leaders provide mature offerings that meet today's market demand. These providers also demonstrate the vision necessary to sustain their leading position as the market evolves. Leaders focus and invest in their offerings in ways that impact and influence the market's overall direction."*

2. Visionaries: *"Visionaries align with the Gartner view of how a market will evolve, but they have less-proven capabilities to deliver against their vision. In new markets, this status is normal. But in more mature markets, it may reflect a competitive strategy for a smaller provider (such as selling innovation ahead of mainstream demand), or a larger provider trying to break out of a rut to differentiate."*

3. Challengers: *"Challengers are well positioned to execute, but may not have a strategy in place to maintain strong, up-to-date value propositions for new customers. Larger providers in mature markets may often be positioned as challengers because they choose to minimize risk. Although challengers typically have significant human and financial resources, they may lack vision, innovation or overall understanding of where the market is headed. In some cases, challengers may offer products that dominate a large but shrinking segment of the market. Challengers have the opportunity to move into the leaders' quadrant by expanding their vision."*

4. Niche Players: *"Niche players do well in a specific market segment or they have limited ability to innovate or outperform other providers. This may be because they focus on a functionality or geographic region, or they are new entrants to the market. Assessing niche players is more challenging than assessing providers in other quadrants. While some niche players could make progress, others do not execute well and may not be able to keep pace with broader market demands."*

According to my interviews with Gartner, buyers should use the Magic Quadrant independently of Gartner's analysts. Furthermore, buyers should not interpret a Magic Quadrant as a recommendation to concentrate on those vendors that appear in the Leader quadrant. Gartner agrees that there is a misconception that being categorized in the Niche quadrant is a bad thing. In fact, a vendor in a non-leader quadrant might be the best vendor for a particular buyer.

The Magic Quadrant Methodology

As has been previously stated, Gartner publishes only a high-level overview as to how it determines the Magic Quadrant rankings. People who read Gartner's analytical products, especially the most influential products, can only review a high-level graphic, which is the output of the research. To find out more details and speak with an analyst, one must pay more, but Gartner does publish the criteria that count toward each axis. These criteria, quoted from Gartner's article *Magic Quadrants and MarketScopes: How Gartner Evaluates Vendors Within a Market,* are listed below.

Orientation of the Magic Quadrant Methodology

Something that was surprising to me (and is surprising to many people the first time I tell them about these criteria) is that only six of the fifteen bullet points above (40%) are in any way related to the actual application offered by the vendor, these are the bullet points with an asterisk in front of them. Only two of the fifteen bullet points above (13.3%) are ***directly*** related to the application. However, these percentages are based simply upon an even weighting of the criteria. Gartner does not explain if they weight the criteria equally or not, so that is all I have to go by for this analysis. After reviewing many Magic Quadrants as part of the research for this book, it does appear as if the criteria are equally weighted.

Completeness of Vision Criterion

1. *"*Market Understanding: The ability of a vendor to understand buyers' needs and translate these needs into products and services. A vendor that shows the highest degree of vision listens and understands buyers' wants and needs, which it can shape or enhance with its vision.*

2. *Marketing Strategy: A clear, differentiated set of messages consistently communicated throughout the organization and publicized through the Web site, advertising, customer programs and positioning statements.*

3. *Sales Strategy: A strategy for selling products that uses the appropriate network of direct and indirect sales, marketing, service and communication affiliates to extend the scope and depth of a vendor's market reach, skills, expertise, technologies, services and customer base.*

4. *Offering (Product) Strategy: A vendor's approach to product development and delivery that relate to current and future requirements.

5. Business Model: The validity and logic of a vendor's underlying business proposition.

6. Vertical/Industry Strategy: A vendor's strategy to direct resources, skills and offerings to meet the needs of market segments, including vertical industries.

7. **Innovation: Marshaling of resources, expertise or capital for competitive advantage, investment, consolidation or defense against acquisition.

8. Geographic Strategy: A vendor's strategy to direct resources, skills and offerings to meet the needs of regions outside of the vendor's 'home' or native area, directly or through partners, channels and subsidiaries, as appropriate for that region and market."

Ability to Execute Criterion

1. **"Product/Service: Core goods and services offered by the vendor that compete in and serve the market. This category includes product and service capabilities, quality, feature sets and skills, offered natively or through original equipment manufacturers, as defined in the market definition and detailed in sub criteria.

2. Overall Viability: Includes an assessment of the vendor's overall financial health, the financial and practical success of the relevant business unit, and the likelihood of that business unit to continue to invest in and offer the product within the vendor's product portfolio.

3. Sales Execution/Pricing: The vendor's capabilities in pre-sales activities and the structure that supports them. This criterion includes deal management, pricing and negotiation, pre-sales support and the overall effectiveness of the sales channel.

4. Market Responsiveness and Track Record: Ability to respond, change direction, be flexible and achieve competitive success as opportunities develop, competitors act, customer needs evolve and market dynamics change. This criterion also considers the vendor's history of responsiveness.

5. *Marketing Execution: The clarity, quality, creativity and efficacy of programs designed to deliver the vendor's message, to influence the market, promote its brand and business, increase awareness of its products and establish a positive identification with the product, brand or vendor with buyers. This 'mind share' can be driven by a combination of publicity, promotions, thought leadership, word of mouth and sales activities.*

6. **Customer Experience: Relationships, products, and services and programs that enable clients to succeed with the products evaluated. This criterion includes the ways customers receive technical support or account support. It can also include ancillary tools, customer support programs (and their quality), availability of user groups and service-level agreements.*

7. **Operations: The vendor's ability to meet its goals and commitments. Factors include the quality of the organizational structure, such as skills, experiences, programs, systems and other vehicles, that enable the vendor to operate effectively and efficiently."*

Gartner is of course free to use any set of criteria that they like. However, I find that few people actually read what their criteria, in fact, are, and most software buyers are under the impression that Gartner's ratings are much more product-focused than they actually are. In fact, most of Gartner's criteria are really just proxies for the size of the software vendor. Therefore, I think that it would be helpful if each Magic Quadrant were published with something like the following disclaimer:

> *"Gartner Magic Quadrants rate vendors on a variety of criteria, 40% of which are related generally to the application, and 13.3% are related directly to the application. For more details on the exact criteria used, see this link."*

Magic Quadrant Scenarios: Large Vendor Versus Small

The following comparison was created to simulate how a large vendor could score well, even if it had very weak software, against a smaller vendor with the best possible rating for its software. To simulate this, I rated all of the product-related criteria as 2 out of 10 for the larger vendor, and 10 out of 10 for the smaller vendor. I then rated the other criteria not related to product such that the larger vendor would score better.

Sample Gartner Magic Quadrant Ranking		Small Vendor A	Large Vendor B
Completeness of Vision Criteria	**Criteria Category**	**Score (1 - 10)**	**Score (1 - 10)**
Market Understanding	*Product	10	5
Marketing Strategy	Marketing	3	8
Sales Strategy	Sales	4	10
Offering (Product) Strategy	*Product	10	2
Business Model	Finance	5	9
Vertical/Industry Strategy	Industry Specialization	6	8
Innovation	Application	10	2
Geographic Strategy	Scale	3	10
Total		*51*	*54*

Ability to Execute	**Criteria Category**	**Score (1 - 10)**	**Score (1 - 10)**
Product/Service	*Product	10	2
Overall Viability	Finance	4	10
Sales Execution/Pricing	Sales	2	9
Market Responsiveness and Track Record	Strategy	3	10
Marketing Execution	Marketing	3	9
Customer Experience	*Product	10	2
Operations	*Multifaceted (But should be counted for the product)	6	7
Total		*38*	*49*

Now we can show how this rating per criteria would show on a Magic Quadrant graphic.

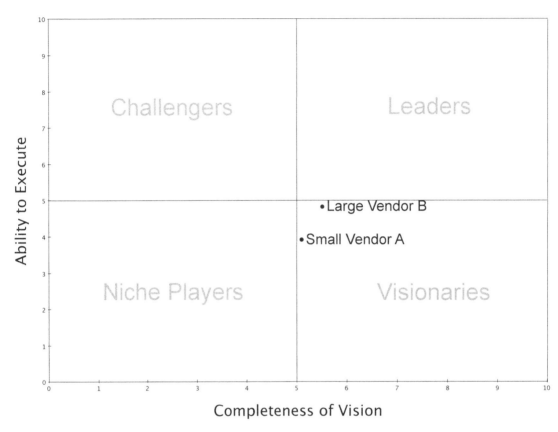

When this hypothetical example is placed on Gartner's Magic Quadrant, the larger vendor scores higher than the smaller vendor. They both would be rated as visionaries, with the larger vendor almost in the leader category.

How can the Magic Quadrant be a correct representation of the scores listed on the previous graphic? A vendor with a score of 2 out of 10 is neither a Visionary nor a Leader. Secondly, a small vendor cannot be considered merely a Visionary simply because it lacks sophistication in sales and marketing. If they score at the top of all product-related criteria, they are the Leader in that product space.

If we look at the scores from the investor's perspective, the low scores outside of the product-related criteria would probably limit the vendor's ability to grow. However, from the software buyer's perspective, clearly the small software vendor would be the preferred choice because their software will implement more easily and have a far higher likelihood of success. However, it does not show that way in the Magic Quadrant.

It should be clear from this Magic Quadrant that the criteria used by a software buyer do not match up very well with the criteria used by Gartner. Something that should also be obvious is that these are very appropriate criteria for rating a company as an investment vehicle, but are not the criteria that one would normally select if one were attempting to develop a matrix for software buyers. However, let's not stop the analysis here. Instead, let's take another example, and in this one the larger vendor has a more competitive product than in the last example.

Sample Gartner Magic Quadrant Ranking		Small Vendor A	Large Vendor B
Completeness of Vision Criteria	**Criteria Category**	**Score (1 - 10)**	**Score (1 - 10)**
Market Understanding	*Product	7	7
Marketing Strategy	Marketing	3	8
Sales Strategy	Sales	4	10
Offering (Product) Strategy	*Product	7	7
Business Model	Finance	5	9
Vertical/Industry Strategy	Industry Specialization	6	8
Innovation	Application	10	2
Geographic Strategy	Scale	3	10
Total		*45*	*61*

Ability to Execute	**Criteria Category**	**Score (1 - 10)**	**Score (1 - 10)**
Product/Service	*Product	7	7
Overall Viability	Finance	4	10
Sales Execution/Pricing	Sales	2	9
Market Responsiveness and Track Record	Strategy	3	10
Marketing Execution	Marketing	3	9
Customer Experience	*Product	7	7
Operations	*Multifaceted (But should be counted for the product)	7	7
Total		*33*	*59*

In this example, we keep all the same values from the first matrix, except this time we make all of the product-related rankings equal, setting them to 7 for both the small vendor and the large vendor.

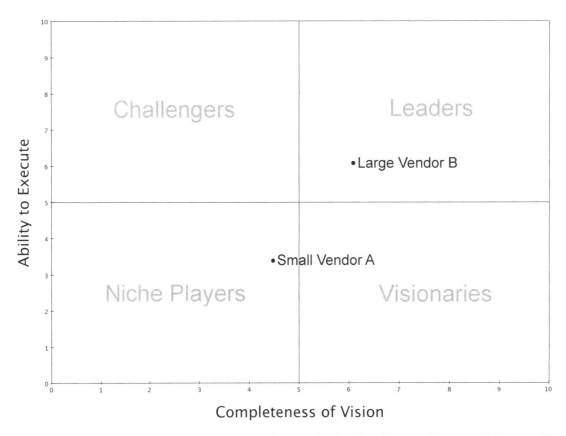

When plotted, we see that the large vendor is now in the Leader quadrant and the smaller vendor is a Niche player. This is true even though they both have the same rating on their product, and by extension would be true if both companies had the exact same product.

Therefore, if a large vendor acquires a smaller vendor, the larger vendor's overall score in the category being analyzed should increase significantly. Is Gartner telling us that it would prefer to have all small software vendors acquired by larger software vendors? Should all software coalesce into mega software vendors? Given the history of larger vendors with software innovation, what would be the predictable outcomes for innovation if this were to occur?

Now let's imagine a smaller vendor that does not spend much on marketing or selling but simply has a great product. Here is one more thought experiment with the Magic Quadrant: How would this smaller vendor with a great product fare in Gartner's rating system?

Sample Gartner Magic Quadrant Ranking		Product Focused Vendor
Completeness of Vision Criteria	**Criteria Category**	**Score (1 - 10)**
Market Understanding	*Product	10
Marketing Strategy	Marketing	1
Sales Strategy	Sales	1
Offering (Product) Strategy	*Product	10
Business Model	Finance	5
Vertical/Industry Strategy	Industry Specialization	5
Innovation	Application	10
Geographic Strategy	Scale	1
Total		*43*

Ability to Execute	**Criteria Category**	**Score (1 - 10)**
Product/Service	*Product	10
Overall Viability	Finance	5
Sales Execution/Pricing	Sales	1
Market Responsiveness and Track Record	Strategy	1
Marketing Execution	Marketing	1
Customer Experience	*Product	10
Operations	*Multifaceted (But should be counted for the product)	5
Total		*33*

In this example, we model a highly product-focused company that invests very little in sales or marketing. However, they have a great product. Criteria that are neither sales nor marketing nor product-focused, we assign an average value of 5. Now let's see how the product-focused company would fare in a Gartner Magic Quadrant.

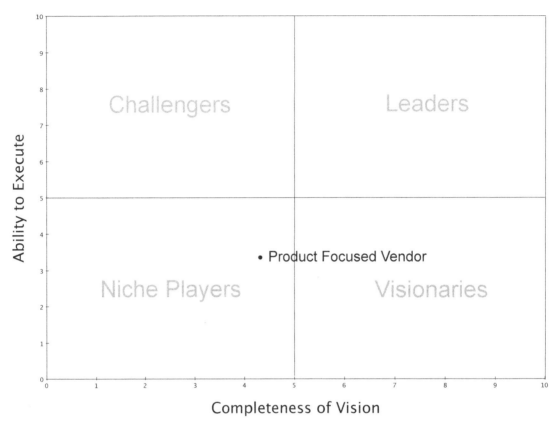

Here we see that the vendor ends up as a Niche player. In Gartner's Magic Quadrant methodology, sales and marketing count for as much in the rating as product-related factors.

Now that we have reviewed sample Magic Quadrants, let's review an actual Magic Quadrant created by Gartner and look at two vendors on opposite sides of the spectrum in terms of both product and size.

Addressing the Product in the Vendor Profile Portion of the Magic Quadrant

In some Magic Quadrants, the product deficiency of the Magic Quadrant methodology is not addressed. However, I found the *Magic Quadrant for Business Intelligence and Analytical Platforms for 2013,* which I use on several occasions in this book because of all the Gartner reports I read, it was the most thorough and clearly addressed the functionality.[10]

- *"Survey data suggests that Birst is the 'new darling' of the Magic Quadrant (like Tableau Software and QlikTech before it). Its customers rated Birst No. 1 in product functionality and customer (that is, product quality, no problems with software, support) and sales experience, with the near-highest or highest scores across all 14 functional areas, performance and ease of use.*

- *Although Birst is a relatively new cloud-based vendor, the platform functionality encompasses all 15 functional areas evaluated in the Magic Quadrant process. Moreover, despite targeting midsize enterprises and departments, the product offers a range of enterprise information management and governance features with integrated data connectivity for a broad range of enterprise applications, data warehouse model autogeneration, and autometadata creation for building a unified semantic layer modeled on top of Birst's relational OLAP (ROLAP) engine and in-memory columnar database (or range of third-party databases, including Oracle, SQL Server, ParAccel, Infobright and so on).*

- *Birst's single front-end user interface for report, ad hoc, dashboard creation, interactive analysis and data discovery is a particularly attractive feature of the platform because it encourages broad use of functionality. Birst customers report among the highest breadth of use of the platform's functionality of any vendor participating in the Magic Quadrant survey. In particular, Birst customers report among the highest percentage of use of static and parameterized reporting, dashboard and interactive visualization functionality of any vendor in the survey."*

However, while Gartner scores Birst extremely high regarding its functionality, it should be no surprise that Birst could get no higher than the Challenger quadrant. See the Magic Quadrant graphic on the following page:

---

[10] When I had this book reviewed by several individuals they asked if I was saying that different Magic Quadrants have different methodologies because I point out the differences between various Magic Quadrant reports. The answer is no. The methodology is the same, but the Magic Quadrants differ a great deal in terms of the level of detail that the Magic Quadrant text explains.

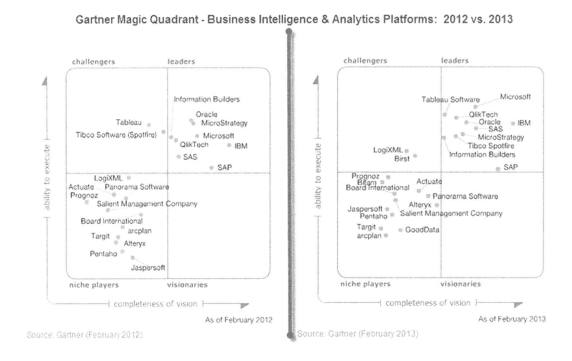

Gartner Magic Quadrant - Business Intelligence & Analytics Platforms: 2012 vs. 2013

Compare Birst to SAP, which is on the opposite side of the continuum from Birst. SAP is a very large and established company. However, it has a weak product in, and a product they acquired called Business Objects back in 2007, which was supposed to be integrated to SAP BW but never actually was integrated. I am very familiar with SAP's business intelligence products because they are implemented on every one of my projects. I see Business Objects much less frequently on my projects, but SAP BW is omnipresent, and never fails to disappoint. SAP BW reports are so late and the productivity of SAP BW is so low that its lack of output is shocking to me. If there is an enterprise application with lower value-added that is as broadly purchased as SAP BW, I would like to know what it is.

Gartner acknowledges the problems in the caution section of the SAP profile for BI, where they state:

> *"When respondents were asked which product-specific limitations*
> *were barriers to wider deployment, more SAP respondents cited*

software quality than for any other vendor. Of all SAP's references, 20.17% cited this limitation, compared with an average of 6.2% across all vendor references. When asked about problems with the software, a greater percentage of SAP references cited 'unreliable, unstable and/or buggy' than for any other vendor in the Magic Quadrant. Much of this poor product quality can be attributed to the challenge of integrating and supporting multiple code bases, such as BW, Web Intelligence, Crystal Reports and Dashboards."

However, there are two very big problems with this analysis. I want to be very specific here because these issues could easily be overlooked.

1. SAP BI/BW[11] has all of these quality problems, which have nothing at all to do with integrating and supporting multiple code bases, such as BW, Web Intelligence, Crystal Reports and Dashboards.

2. What Gartner is referring to here is primarily the integration of the products from the Business Objects acquisition. It is well-known in the industry that SAP has done a bad job with Business Objects. Ever since Business Objects was acquired by SAP, the product has stagnated, prices have gone up, and customer support has declined; in other words, it has been a standard software vendor acquisition. However, this report was written in 2013. Let us remember that Business Objects was acquired in 2007. Shouldn't SAP have ironed out the integration by this point? Why is Gartner cutting SAP such an enormous amount of slack for a blown acquisition that SAP can't get right six years down the road? Finally, if it is not right after six years, when can we expect it to be right?

3. Gartner is combining several issues, which will only serve to confuse buyers as to the nature of the issues with SAP's Business Intelligence offerings. Buyers cannot make good decisions when such basic cause and effect is confused in this manner.

Gartner goes on to criticize SAP for its support.

---

[11] SAP's BI product is referred to as both BI and BW—a remnant of an unsuccessful product name change. SAP tried to get BW (Business Warehouse) renamed to BI, but then reversed itself.

> *"In addition to poor product quality, customers have complained about unsatisfactory support. In our latest survey, SAP ranked last in customer experience and sales experience. Unfortunately for SAP customers, it isn't a matter of just one bad year, because SAP has consistently ranked at or near the bottom of customer support since Gartner started this series of surveys in 2008."*

This is exactly what I have experienced during projects as well, so Gartner is in line with my consulting experiences. They go on to say the following:

> *"When compared with other vendors in the survey, SAP scored below average across all 15 BI platform capabilities evaluated during the Magic Quadrant research process."*

I agree with this as well. BI is an extremely weak application.

If one looks at the items listed under the strengths area of the SAP profile in this report, most of the items are related to either SAP's size (they are the top deployed vendor in the world), or to positive predictions for the future. However, how can a vendor with the serious quality and customer service problems that SAP has in Business Intelligence, be listed in the leader category in this space? Granted they are just barely a Leader, but they are still in the Leader category. On the other hand, SAP is the largest vendor by sales in the Business Intelligence space, so does that simple fact alone make them a Leader? Some may say the largest vendor by software sales is the leader, no matter what the quality of the product. It's not a simple question to answer. A marketing person would say SAP is the leader, but a product person like myself would choke at putting SAP high in a Magic Quadrant for Business Intelligence.

Obviously this issue comes down to how the methodology is designed. The methodology, as much as the virtues of each vendor or product, determine the position in the Magic Quadrant or any of Gartner's other analytical products.

Pricing as Criteria, but for Whom?

Several of the criteria are confusing in terms of how they would be rated, or which way they should be rated. One such confusing criterion is price. Is Gartner rating the vendor's pricing from the perspective of the vendor, buyer or investor? I ask because the interests for pricing are not aligned; a price that is good for the vendor is not best for the buyer. For instance, a large vendor will typically charge more than a smaller vendor. This extra charge is good for the vendor and investor, but not so good for the buyer. Of course, if the price becomes too high, it can eventually become bad for the vendor and the investor. High prices can drive down business and may not be what economists refer to as the "profit maximizing price" (the profit maximizing price is not the highest possible price, but the price which maximizes the profit as a consequence of a high price and a high volume). This is one of the problems with attempting to use a single matrix to represent multiple interests. Gartner is cagey about how it rates price. If Gartner published how each vendor scored on the pricing criteria, I could evaluate and determine how Gartner rates vendors on price. But they don't, so it remains a gray area.

Gartner's Large Vendor Bias

In its website and other documentation, Gartner repeatedly makes the point that they are wholly objective. As an IT consultant with many years of experience, I can say unequivocally that the most innovative products do not come from the larger software vendors. The most innovative vendors I know of are small, and in fact, the larger vendors tend to focus more on marketing and sales than on software innovation. This topic is covered in the link below.

http://www.scmfocus.com/enterprisesoftwarepolicy/2012/03/11/why-the-largest-enterprise-software-companies-have-no-reason-to-innovate/

When larger software vendors are allowed to purchase smaller software vendors they frequently do so simply to eliminate a competitor and to acquire their customers. This is explained in detail in the article link below.

http://www.scmfocus.com/enterprisesoftwarepolicy/2012/01/02/why-ibm-should-not-be-allowed-to-acquire-software-companies/

However, the largest software vendors are consistently ranked highest by Gartner, even where the larger vendors have marginal products and the smaller vendors have products that are clearly superior.

The Specifics of a Large Vendor Bias

Let me state exactly what I mean by a "large vendor bias": if identical software existed in two different vendors, where one of the vendors was larger than the other, the larger vendor would be rated higher in the software category than the smaller vendor.

I want to point out that I don't think it's possible to rank anything without having some type of bias. People tend to be very uncomfortable around the term "bias," but they really shouldn't be, because bias is near universal. For instance, if I created a Magic Quadrant for any category of software, my Magic Quadrant would have the vendors in very different positions from Gartner's. This is because my bias is to focus on the application and to look at other factors as secondary. To me, focusing on the application does not seem like a bias because I truly believe this is the most important consideration to software selection and implementation. However, from another person's vantage point, I have a bias. Gartner itself states on its website that it is unbiased, and in fact, the header on the SCM Focus website includes the words "Unbiased Explanations of SCM Software." So, while being unbiased is, of course, the goal of any analyst, it's not really possible. What I can say is that SCM Focus does not have financial bias, because the articles are free and I am not paid by vendors or anyone else to write them. However, financial bias is certainly only one of the many types of bias.

In Chapter 9 of the book *Supply Chain Forecasting Software* (which is a chapter dedicated to the study of bias), I analyze bias removal. This was a very interesting area of study, partially because of the enormous discrepancy between the reality of bias and the interpretation of bias. Humans have so many areas of bias, including any type of perception or forecasting.[12] For instance, humans have a well-known

---

[12] I have left out the bias of the sense organs so as not to digress too far afield. However, through evolution humans have developed sense organs that perceive some stimuli and not others. Dogs, depending upon the breed, have a nose that is between 1,000 to 10,000 times more powerful than a human's; however, their eyesight is considerably less powerful. Bias actually begins at the sensory organs, and reflects what evolution decided to develop for that organism, choosing some capabilities over others.

optimism bias. There is confirmation bias—the selective use of information to support what one already believes to be true and rejecting information that contradicts one's hypothesis. These are the unconscious biases that are part of the human condition. Then we get into social and institutional biases. In studying the bias of financial analysts for the book *Supply Chain Forecasting Software*, I found a detailed explanation of how analysts biased their forecasts to achieve career advancement. A good example of forecast bias, which is produced by institutional financial incentives, is described below:

> *"Sell-side analysts are pressured to issue optimistic forecasts and recommendations for several reasons. First, their compensation is tied to the amount of trade they generate for their brokerage firms. Given widespread unwillingness or inability to sell short, more trade will result from a 'buy' than from a 'sell' recommendation. Second, a positive outlook improves the chances of analysts' employers winning investment banking deals. Third, being optimistic has historically helped analysts obtain inside information from the firms they cover. While all these pressures introduce an optimistic bias to analysts' views, the magnitude of the bias is held in check by reputational concerns. Ultimately, an analyst's livelihood—the ability to generate trades and attract investment banking business—depends on her credibility."*
>
> —Anna Scherbina

> *"Analysts will set the optimistic bias at an optimal point that balances the benefit of being upbeat against the cost to their reputation."*
>
> —Anna Scherbina

Here the case is made that financial forecasters must trade off pressures to create optimistic forecasts with their concerns for their reputations. In this way, the forecast of a financial analyst can be seen as less of a forecast and more of a balancing act; they attempt to develop numbers that garner favor with the powerful companies from whom the analysts' investment banks gain business, while keeping some semblance of credibility with investors. This "credibility" also determines whether "information channels" are kept open or closed and highlights how political factors can influence a financial analyst's forecast.

We hear the term "unbiased" quite frequently. However, when one analyzes the output of individuals and institutions, we find bias to be universal. The best that can be hoped for is that financial bias is reduced—but even this is incredibly rare. Here I would like to borrow from noted philosopher and linguist Noam Chomsky, who said, *"Everyone has a bias, the honest people tell you what their bias is. People that are not honest say they have no bias."*

How the Large Vendor Bias Is Introduced

I am convinced that Gartner does not alter the numbers in its reports, but rather that Gartner selects a methodology that has the intended outcome of benefiting larger and more established vendors. Repeated observations of this outcome from a wide variety of Gartner reports make this conclusion unavoidable. However, it is unclear if this bias is due (either completely or partially) to the money paid by the largest vendors, or if Gartner is simply representing the interests of large buyers who tend to want to buy their software from larger vendors. Gartner knows its market very well, so it may simply be that Gartner has modeled their methodology based upon the criteria that large buyers themselves look for. To software-oriented people such as myself, the functionality of the application is the main focus, but to large corporations it is not the focus. Many other factors play into their decision.

Here are some interesting comments on the topic, and these quotations give insight into the objectivity of Gartner.

> *"On Magic Quadrants perception is reality. Go look at the 40 to 50 Magic Quadrants you issue and see how few smaller, innovative vendors show up on top right. You have the data points—but with so many markets going through rapid change it rewards established vendors far longer than it should because they are more 'viable.' Time to question the MQ methodology. I would say...at the firm level Gartner looks like a mouthpiece for larger vendors."*—Vinnie Mirchandani

"The biggest potential trap for you with this MQ is Gartner's continued over-weighting of 'name' vendors. It is only a slight overstatement to say that the bigger the software vendor, the weaker their tool. It's been that way for more than a decade. This does not mean that only small vendors and open source projects can create great Web CMS packages. Larger vendors just seem to lack the agility and interest to keep up. It's not a big market, and their attention lies elsewhere.

This has real consequences for you if you select a tool based on putative staying power or supposed platform consistency of an IBM, Open Text, Oracle, Microsoft, or Autonomy. For some bitter history here, you have only to look at the train-wrecks that were implementations of EMC's now deprecated WCM products. Customers bought EMC's web content management tools for a variety of reasons: perceived platform consistency, the free licenses thrown into document management mega-deals, and last but not least: favorable analyst reviews. Many of these implementations became failures of epic proportions, sometimes with career-stifling consequences for project leaders (but alas, rarely any blowback for the people who recommended the tool). This is serious stuff, folks."—Tony Byrne of Real Story

I have had several conversations with people at Gartner (years before I decided to write this book) during which they repeatedly stated that they believe they have a reputation for being objective. However, this subject is much grayer than Gartner would have it according to my conversations with many people and from publicly-available information on the Internet. Questions of bias plague Gartner, but it should be understood that this conversation is held chiefly among those who are the most sophisticated in their understanding of Gartner—usually those who work in marketing within vendors. Among investors and software buyers, the controversy regarding Gartner's bias is not prevalent. In fact, among the individuals who are executive decision makers in software buyers, I do not see the topic as even a minor point of conversation.

It would be good if Gartner had more defenders than current or ex-Gartner analysts only. I have observed that the more experienced and savvy the individual, the less he or she is convinced that Gartner is objective. Those who are most critical of Gartner's objectivity are those who work for the best-of-breed vendors or smaller vendors.

I can say with confidence that this criticism is not sour grapes on the part of these individuals, who are with smaller vendors belonging to the software category in which I specialize. I have used the software of these vendors as well as the software of the larger software vendors, and in each case the software of these smaller vendors is far superior to software offered by the larger vendors (which, as stated previously, is ranked by Gartner higher than that from these smaller vendors). Vendors that provide "specific point solutions," (something which is considered a negative but really should not be) have a legitimate complaint in that the Gartner methodologies favor both large vendors and vendors with broad suites.

The ways in which Gartner shows a preference for large vendors are listed below:

1. A number of the criteria in the Magic Quadrant specifically give an advantage to large vendors over smaller vendors.

2. Gartner prefers software vendors that are diversifying their portfolio and have broad offerings. Gartner places "suites" of products into Magic Quadrants, making it impossible for smaller vendors to perform well. For example, no Magic Quadrant exists for production planning software. If a vendor only made production planning software, how could they ever perform well in a general supply chain planning Magic Quadrant, designed to rate a suite of software? I have also seen buyers make enormous mistakes buying production planning software and demand planning software because the products were part of the suite of a large vendor. The supply chain planning Magic Quadrant score led these buyers to completely over-estimate the ability of the applications in the suite. Gartner may say that these buyers should have spent more time and money leveraging Gartner analysts to get a fuller picture of the specific software within the suite.

3. Gartner sometimes places revenue cutoffs that exclude many smaller vendors from the Magic Quadrant. The revenue cutoff meets the needs of

their clients in some cases and reduces the number of companies for which a full analysis must be performed, but obviously it shows a preference for the larger vendors in a category. I know some fantastic software companies that are great software buys, but which have low revenues.

4. Gartner will rate vendors in categories for which they do not have products, under the logic that they *will* have a product.

5. Gartner focuses some analytical products on small vendors and emerging technologies (Magic Quadrants are for stable technologies), most notably Cool Vendors; however, these are not anywhere close to as influential with decision makers as the Magic Quadrant. The most likely explanation for the existence of these types of awards is to maintain the technology advisor services revenue that it receives from smaller vendors.

6. A vendor can have the lowest quality software and lowest support in a software category (as with SAP with the BI Magic Quadrant) and still find itself in the Leader quadrant (although not highly rated in the Leader quadrant) based upon software revenues and vendor size.

7. As with most of the business media, Gartner writes articles on acquisitions of smaller vendors by larger vendors that are primarily positive. Gartner essentially writes from the perspective of the acquiring vendor. Anti-competitive issues or the reduction in innovation (both of which have repeatedly been demonstrated as the natural consequences of acquisitions in the software area) is not Gartner's focus. I have never read a single report by Gartner on acquisitions that also explains that costs tend to rise while support tends to decline, as the product being acquired tends to stagnate. Gartner does not point out to its readers that many acquisitions have *nothing to do with acquiring software,* but are about acquiring customers and knocking out a competitor. For Gartner, size means more financial resources and more stability. Either Gartner has an exceedingly simplistic understanding of the broader competitive issues that are brought to the enterprise software area by mergers, or they are so captured by the influence of larger vendors that expressing a more nuanced analysis is of no interest to them. For example, I have written articles stating that it is clearly past the time where the Federal Trade Commission (FTC) investigates SAP for anti-competitive

market practices. I have also provided a large pool of evidence that the FTC could work from in order to assist in these regards (see the article link below). However, Gartner will never publish this type of article.

http://www.scmfocus.com/enterprisesoftwarepolicy/2011/11/19/the-case-against-sap-for-anti-trust-violations/

There are four main reasons that can be reasonably given for Gartner's large vendor bias.

1. Large vendors can pay more in consulting fees and for events than smaller vendors.

2. Larger vendors can allocate more people to working with Gartner and to knowing how to present the vendor's products to Gartner. The book *Up and to the Right*—which shows software vendors how to get high rankings—is at least some evidence that a high ranking is not based simply upon the quality of a vendor's software or "vision."

3. Most of the smaller software vendors are also much younger than the large software vendors and are simply not savvy to the analysts' game.

4. Gartner appears to base its research upon the preferences of the large buyers that are its core market, causing it to design its methodologies such that larger vendors perform better, independent of the actual software.

Taking Gartner's Bias into Account

How much each factor plays into this large vendor bias is unknown and would be difficult to demonstrate. However, for those seeking to adjust the ratings, the main point is that bias occurs and is clearly noticeable. Therefore, when reviewing a Gartner report or a Magic Quadrant, it is a logical practice to "adjust" the larger vendors down from where Gartner has them ranked. How much exactly is difficult to say; it's not a perfect science. If Gartner published the specific ratings per criteria it would be easier to remove the criteria that are unimportant to buyers and more relevant for investors, and vice versa. However, Gartner does not do that, so all that can be stated reliably is that Gartner overrates the large vendors.

Gartner's IT Versus Business Bias

Within buyers, Gartner's reports also have multiple categories of customers, the two most prominent being IT and the business. IT tends to be pro-Gartner because IT does not like to deal with many vendors, many service contracts, etc. Therefore, IT has been one of the ***main proponents of purchasing software from fewer vendors.*** This policy is intended to alleviate the costs associated with application integration, and was one of the primary arguments used to promote the sale of ERP systems. However, integration costs as a percentage of IT budgets did not decline after the purchase of more "integrated" systems. This is a fact that has eluded not only almost every IT analyst, but software buyers as well and is covered in detail in my book *The Real Story Behind ERP: Separating Fact from Fiction.*[13] While ineffective at reducing the costs of integration, this approach of buying from fewer vendors has numerous downsides with respect to implementation success. For instance, when a company restricts its buying alternatives to fewer software vendors, the business loses because no single vendor offers the best solution for even a small fraction of the software categories. What makes a solution the "best solution" is not only the general functionality of an application, but includes how buying from more software vendors makes available to the business more applications that are suited to its industry and to the requirements of the particular buying company.

---

[13] The initial idea behind ERP systems was that it would combine many different applications into a single system, thus reducing application integration issues. However, after the major ERP vendors sold the ERP product into companies, they began to develop specialized products for things like supply chain planning, business intelligence, customer relationship management, etc. This was done for several reasons. First, there was simply no way that an ERP system with its elementary approach to all functionality (with the possible exception of finance and accounting) could meet all the needs of companies. Secondly, once ERP companies had sold their ERP applications, they needed to develop more applications in order to grow their sales. Once they had the ERP system implemented, they had the network effect on their side as the ERP system is the "mother ship application"—the application or set of applications to which all other applications must integrate. Thus they were in a competitive position to sell more software into these accounts. These applications all have their own platforms and have adapters to one another, but each are a separate application, with a different database and sitting on different hardware, meaning that companies are essentially back where they started before the move to ERP systems. Except, they now rely more on external application development through commercial software rather than internal application development. All of these factors undercut one of the primary arguments that were often used to sell ERP systems: that they would reduce costs. More on this topic can be read here: http://www.scmfocus.com/scmhistory/2013/06/how-the-original-logic-fo-erp-systems-turned-out-to-be-false/

Thus, a mix of competing interests makes decisions that are not necessarily based on evidence, but upon which department or grouping has the most power within the buying company. For whatever reason, during the last several decades, IT has tended to get its way more often than not in software selection.

How Gartner Pushes Buyers Toward More Expensive Solutions

Gartner also tends to push buyers toward more expensive solutions. This higher expense is not only for software, but also for services. For instance, I work as an SAP consultant, and SAP consultants are some of the most expensive resources in IT. One aspect of the cost is the hourly billing rate, which is high. Another aspect is that SAP software is complicated to install, so SAP projects tend to be quite long. The billing rate multiplied by the total number of hours is of course, the consulting cost. The extent to which the cost to implement SAP is higher than to implement "best-of-breed solutions" is shown in the articles below. In these articles (knowing that I would receive a great deal of negative feedback), I provided an advantage to SAP by setting their software costs to zero.[14]

http://www.scmfocus.com/supplyplanning/2011/09/17/what-if-you-paid-nothing-for-sap-software-how-saps-tco-compares-for-supply-planning/

http://www.scmfocus.com/productionplanningandscheduling/2011/08/09/what-if-you-paid-nothing-for-sap-software-how-saps-tco-compares-for-production-planning/

In terms of the overall costs, the implementation consulting costs far exceed the cost to purchase the product. (Therefore, it makes little sense to simply focus on the cost of acquiring software. Instead a total cost approach, which includes implementation and maintenance costs, makes the most sense.) These consulting resources can come from the software vendor or from a consulting company. The software that is selected in large part determines the cost of the consulting that will follow. The differences in the total costs between large vendors and small vendors are quite significant, which is why placing them in the same category is problematic. This would be as

---

[14] SAP is a very powerful influence in IT and has many people that make a very good living from working in SAP. Unless my research results are heavily skewed in favor of SAP, I can expect negative feedback on my articles.

if *Consumer Reports* placed Lexus automobiles in the same category as Toyota's automobiles.[15] Lexus would outscore all of the Toyota products because Lexus uses upgraded components, paint, engines, etc. However, obviously Toyota sells many more cars than Lexus because price is an important consideration in the decision to buy an automobile. This is intuitively obvious: different priced items should be compared in different categories. If I am looking for an automobile and my budget is twenty thousand dollars, I am quite aware that a forty thousand dollar car is probably better. I wouldn't care so much as that car is out of my price range. If the costs of acquisition—as well as implementation and maintenance—were included in some type of "value matrix," the matrix would look quite a bit different and the larger vendors would drop significantly in the rankings.

While Gartner's Magic Quadrant rankings do not account for cost, sometimes the vendor descriptions do. For instance, in the *Magic Quadrant for Business Intelligence and Analytical Platforms for 2013,* which must be one of the longest and most thorough Gartner reports ever written, costs are discussed in several vendor profiles. The following quotations are examples [emphasis is mine]:

- *"Licensing cost remains a concern. When references were asked what limits wider deployment,* **37.78% indicated the cost of the software, compared with the industry average of 25.4% across all vendor references.**

- *When compared with Actuate, Quiterian has some concerns,* **including cost,** *ease of use for business users, ease of use for developers, support quality and product quality, all ranked below the survey average."*

Using a Software Vendor's Sales Strategy and Business Model

Numerous parts of the Magic Quadrant methodology should be relevant to corporate software buyers. For instance, the following quotation from Mike Whitehorn of *The Register* is instructive.

> *"So, Gartner collects a huge amount of valuable information; in analytical terms, it collects data over 15 different dimensions. But to produce the MQ (Magic Quadrant) it then proceeds to amalgamate seven of the evaluation criteria into one dimension (ability to execute)*

---

[15] Anyone who reads *Consumer Reports* will know that luxury cars and SUVs are in their own category.

and the remaining eight into another (completeness of vision). Fifteen dimensions of data are collapsed into two.

This is where the problem lies and is best illustrated by an example. Two of the initial criteria Gartner uses are Sales Strategy and Business Model. Suppose that a company develops a world-class sales strategy. As it turns out, by error, this strategy fatally compromises its business model. This was clearly a poor choice (but let's face it, one that has been made by several computer companies) and you would probably wish to avoid investing in the company's products."

It is unclear why a software buyer should be concerned about the software vendor's sales strategy. They should care about the vendor's business model in terms of its ability to stay in business. However, this can be estimated by some type of risk metric, which I would argue should be kept separate—something which Gartner does with its vendor rating. Certainly it is convenient for Gartner to have one Magic Quadrant, but the question should first be whether it makes any sense. This provides the distinct impression that the Magic Quadrant is directed partially toward investors. In fact, it turns out that investors are a source of subscribers for Gartner, as noted by the following quotation from Louis Columbus writing for *Commerce Times.*

"Investors came to expect Gartner's figures in S1s and business plans. These expectations drove many start-ups into subscribing with Gartner and other research firms when they really could not afford it. This dynamic alone helped lift Gartner's Magic Quadrant to Holy-Grail status in the vendor community."

However, the interests of investors and the interests of software buyers are not one and the same, so to have a methodology that attempts to combine the interests of both is difficult to navigate.

Using The Reference ability of Customers

The quality and quantity of customer references is clearly an important criterion. However, Gartner downgrades a vendor if they *lack globally-reference-able customers,* clearly providing a bias for larger software vendors. Usually smaller software vendors do not sell out of their home country/region until they reach a certain size. Selling out of the home country/region means either developing reseller partnerships with foreign consulting firms or opening offices in other regions. It's quite a big step and—because it involves more risk—it's not one that makes a lot of sense until a company has reached a certain size. Cloud software vendors are particularly well-positioned to grow globally with lower risk, but at the time of this publication cloud vendors are still only a small portion of the overall enterprise vendor marketplace. Getting back to the main point, it creates an unequal playing field if the lack of global references counts against a software vendor. I know of several smaller vendors with far superior products to the largest vendors in the world, and I would not think of letting their lack of global reach lead me to downgrade them as a vendor. This is echoed by Louis Columbus in his article for *Commerce Times.*

> *"It's fairly common to see the industry's largest IT companies in the Leader Quadrant, and that's because these firms with the most resources have the ability to execute on a global scale. But what is lost in the Quadrant are the vendors with agility, responsiveness and close alignment with their customers' needs."*

I completely agree with this quotation. My implementation experience has taught me that software vendor size does not lead to either quality software or higher implementation success, and that most of the best applications and best values reside with the smaller software vendors.

Problems with the Magic Quadrant's Specificity

Gartner does not produce Magic Quadrants for every software category or for every area. For instance, in my software category, there is no Magic Quadrant for production planning, demand planning or supply planning. These are all subcategories of the software category "supply chain planning," and Gartner does have a Magic Quadrant for this broader category. However, when a Magic Quadrant does not exist for the subcategory that a buyer is interested in purchasing, it does not work to use a Magic Quadrant for the broader category. Beyond this, I did not actually find articles (not only Magic Quadrants, but any articles whatsoever) on production planning or supply planning, which are major subcategories of software within the supply chain planning category. The best analogy that I can give is that—while Honda may be a very good brand—one cannot actually buy a Honda. One must buy a Honda Accord or a Honda Odyssey. As good as Hondas are, people want to see the model compared against models from competing brands. By the same extension, it makes little sense to try to determine which demand planning application scores highest in Gartner's Magic Quadrant, as brought up in the following quote by Mark Madsen. Here he is talking about a different software category, but the same issue applies.

> *"How can someone take seriously 'IBM' or 'Oracle' in the quadrant? Which of the dozen or so products from a single vendor is implied for leadership? If it stated 'Oracle Data Integration' or 'IBM's DataMirror' it would be more useful. Some vendor's products are DOA while others are terrific. Since the evaluation is not the products but the vendors, it's not possible to use the MQ to choose DI technology appropriate to the situation. When I'm with clients who are Gartner subscribers I have to guide them in their use of these results."*

Getting back to the supply chain planning category, I can say that no vendor rates highly across all of the software subcategories of supply chain planning. Secondly, some software vendors work better than others for certain requirements, and some for certain industries over others. Making broad Magic Quadrants, such as the one for supply chain planning, will tend to drive potential buyers to review the larger software vendors that have the broadest range of software within the software category. For instance, here is a quotation from Gartner's Magic Quadrant write up on supply chain planning.

> *"SAP has a stronger focus that Oracle on business process and a well-established, capable platform in Advanced Planning and Optimization (APO), which covers all the functional areas of supply chain planning, according to Payne. But SAP APO lacks depth in inventory optimization and production scheduling."*

I have written five books on SAP's supply chain planning suite. When looking at the previous quote, it's hard to see what it is attempting to accomplish, but the statement certainly benefits SAP. SAP's supply chain planning suite (called APO) has roughly ten modules (depending upon how you count them)—some are mature and implemented at many companies, some are quite immature and barely implemented anywhere. Each module must be evaluated independently. There is no way to cover the suite with such a high level explanation of how it works. In fact, one of the worst things a company could do is to try to find a single vendor for all of its advanced planning needs as it would leave major areas of requirements unaddressed and would oversimplify the decision-making toward vendor-oriented criteria rather than application-oriented criteria. This is where the analyst comes in; however, I question the point of even having a supply chain planning Magic Quadrant if it is so broad that it cannot be used for specific application purchase decisions, and if it promotes purchasing behavior that looks for suites—a bad value for buyers.

Conclusion

The Magic Quadrant is a simple and well-known graphic, and is the best-known research produced by Gartner. The Magic Quadrant results in a vendor being placed in one of four specific quadrants which is either a Leader, Visionary, Challengers, or Niche Player. Neither the Magic Quadrant nor any of Gartner's other research products are designed to be used without also purchasing Gartner's services and therefore speaking with a Gartner analyst. Gartner publishes only a high-level overview as to how it determines the Magic Quadrant rankings. Many people that use the Magic Quadrant for decision making in their purchases do not fully read the Magic Quadrant, and do not know Magic Quadrant's methodology, which is unfortunate, because understanding the methodology typically changes the interpretation of the Magic Quadrant. In fact, most of Gartner's criteria are really just proxies for the size of the software vendor. In order to demonstrate this feature of the Magic Quadrant, an exercise was performed in this chapter to explain how much impact the size of the vendor would have on their score. Some of the analysis provided with respect to Gartner's Magic Quadrant is contradictory, and the example I give of this is the rather hazy Magic Quadrant criterion of pricing. The vendor, buyer and investor all have different interests when it comes to pricing, so whose interests are prioritized in the Magic Quadrant? This is one of the problems with attempting to use a single matrix to represent multiple interests.

Gartner and various Gartner defenders—which are typically ex-Gartner analysts, propose that there is vendor bias based upon vendor size, however, this is simply impossible, as the exercise in this chapter on the Magic Quadrant should have demonstrated beyond a shadow of a doubt. However, further evidence is provided by the fact that Gartner frequently publishes Magic Quadrants for suites, for which is it not possible for smaller vendors that only have one or a few of the products in the suite to score well. This is true regardless of the quality of their individual products. Because of the large vendor bias of Gartner, and the fact that large vendors have a strong tendency to have higher overall total costs of ownership, following the advice of Gartner will tend to lead an inflation of costs for IT purchases, and an inflation of the overall IT budget. Because Gartner promotes larger vendors at the expense of smaller vendors, placing the emphasis of the software selection on vendor size over software functionality, Gartner does a much better job meeting the purchasing needs of IT rather than the business within buying companies.

CHAPTER 6

Other Analytical Products Offered by Gartner

While the Magic Quadrant is the most popular analytical product offered by Gartner, it is only one of several. Other products are described in the following pages, and the definitions of these analytical products are from Gartner's website.

Hype Cycles

"Gartner Hype Cycles provide a graphic representation of the maturity and adoption of technologies and applications, and how they are potentially relevant to solving real business problems and exploiting new opportunities. Gartner Hype Cycle methodology gives you a view of how a technology or application will evolve over time, providing a sound source of insight to manage its deployment within the context of your specific business goals."

This is probably one of the more amusing (in a good way) of Gartner's products. The Hype Cycle, for which there is a book written, describes the reality of technology—essentially the broad applicability of any technology. This is some combination of how new technologies are marketed versus the more difficult work in actually implementing and gaining user acceptance and competence in the technology. Essentially the Hype Cycle estimates where in the lifecycle of a technology is presently so that executives in buying companies can make their investments in a technology. It is also used by investors to time investments.

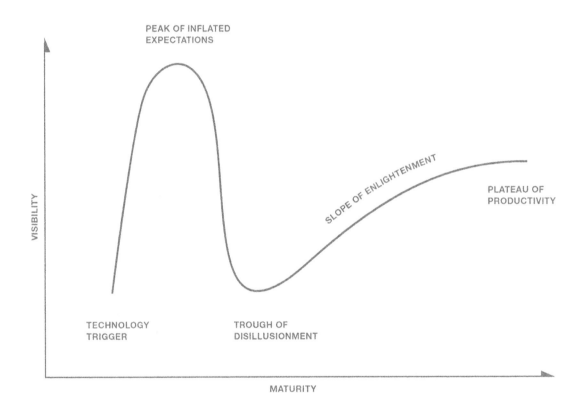

Marketscopes

> *"When markets are growing and IT solutions are stable, Magic Quadrants provide the best tool for understanding how the players are competitively positioned. But when new markets emerge and user requirements are in flux, solutions are often approached in wildly different ways, making a competitive positioning less useful. Mature markets present a similar challenge, as the differentiators among*

*consolidating technology providers and solutions grow more difficult
to discern."*

I find Gartner's Marketscopes fill out my picture of the software category. This
is, in fact, the real strength of the Gartner analysts, as they have a good understanding of the composition of the market. Marketscopes rate the market as well
as the vendors in the software market. Marketscopes essentially tell the corporate
buyers how good their options are.

Vendor Ratings

*"Clients use our well-defined methodology to rate IT technology
providers—large, small, public or private. Gartner Vendor Ratings
assess all the different aspects of a technology provider, such as its
strategy, organization, products, technology, marketing, financials
and support. These ratings are periodically revised to reflect changes
in assessment when a significant internal or external event directly
affects the provider."*

This is not so much an evaluation of the products of the vendor as the vendor itself.
The rating system for vendors is much like the ratings that financial analysts
give stocks. Gartner uses five categories to rate vendors: Strong Positive, Positive,
Promising, Caution, Strong Negative. This rating clearly benefits larger vendors
that are more established and have more resources. Of course, when a buyer is
going to make a purchase decision from a particular vendor, it makes sense to
perform some more analysis on that vendor. I do not find that Vendor Ratings are
used often in procurement decisions. Furthermore, because the Magic Quadrant
contains so many vendor-related criteria, it seems this analytical product is
somewhat redundant.

Market Forecasts

*"Our Market Forecasts use primary surveys, inquiry analysis and
secondary sources to help you fully understand a market's future
spending pattern. We cover a broad supply chain—from raw
materials to semiconductors, to systems, software and services.
Gartner forecasts provide two years of history while peering five years*

into the future. You get a comprehensive understanding of supply and demand by market, country and global region."

This research is often repeated out on the Internet and is helpful in understanding not only the forecasts, but also the size of various markets. For instance, Gartner estimates the current level and the growth in overall IT spending. This analytical product is useful for investors.

Market Share Analysis

"Understanding market share is one of the most important metrics used by executives in any business. Through our Market Share Analysis methodology, clients see how share is allocated among 400 technology providers in 37 key markets. Our detailed analysis of how provider revenue is allocated reveals what types of solutions are succeeding, which are trailing and where opportunities exist for providers to take additional share."

This one is self-explanatory. In addition to being useful to buyers, this analytical product is useful for investors and vendors as well. Investors can make investment decisions, for instance, by looking for trends in market share. Vendors can review their competitive position by understanding the market share in both the software categories that they currently compete in, as well as the market share of various vendors in software categories they are thinking of entering.

Market Updates

This is not a specifically-named product by Gartner, but Gartner routinely writes reports that describe the state of different software categories. Gartner's market updates provide much more detail and analysis than is generally available from the Internet. Market updates are one of my favorite Gartner offerings. As a researcher, Gartner's press releases—which do not require a Gartner subscription—help quantify changes in the marketplace. For instance, I was recently performing research on ERP SaaS providers, and found Gartner's webpage naming NetSuite as the fastest growing global financial software management vendor. (Interestingly, they did not use the term ERP, although that is how NetSuite classifies itself.)

http://www.netsuite.com/portal/press/releases/nlpr05-13-13.shtml?inid=
gartner

This short article contained some extremely interesting information.

1. *"NetSuite's 2012 global growth rate of 49 percent was entirely organic, significantly outperforming its closest competitors, some of whom relied on acquisitions to gain customers."*

2. *"NetSuite is the only pure cloud company among the Top 15 global FMS vendors."*

3. *"NetSuite's growth rate was more than four times the growth rates of legacy competitors combined."*

4. *"NetSuite's growth continues to build upon prior successes as its overall share of the global FMS market jumped to number 12."*

These were all valuable pieces of information. Gartner excels at this broad-scale type of market analysis, especially when reflecting on something that has already happened.

Conclusion

This book is primarily about Gartner as a company and the Magic Quadrant analytical product, but I wanted to cover Gartner's other offerings as well. Although this was not an exhaustive listing of what they offer, this chapter covered some of the most popular of Gartner's offerings aside from the Magic Quadrant.

The Hype Cycle is essentially designed to keep buying companies (as well as investors) from investing in new technologies before they are mature. It is an inspired, and tongue in cheek offering that allows companies to time their new technology purchases. The Hype Cycle is a prediction, however, not all new technologies mature to a useful stage, so the product has its limitations. Vendor Ratings allow a buying company to learn more about a vendor prior to a software purchase and emphasizes the fact that software purchases create a long term relationship between the buyer and the seller. Market Forecasts are directed toward investors who use it to review the attractiveness of various markets for their investment dollars. Another analytical product that can be useful for buyers, but is more useful to investors is the Market Share Analysis. I believe that the Market Share Analysis is the most comprehensive of its type for markets that Gartner covers. Gartner's market updates essentially communicate changes in the enterprise space marketplace and seem to be designed to attract attention to Gartner and to keep their name relevant and known outside of simply those that pay for subscriptions.

CHAPTER 7

Gartner's Future and Cloud Computing

In Gartner's annual report, they mention the risks that they face.

> *"We face direct competition from a significant number of independent providers of information products and services, including information available on the Internet free of charge. We also compete indirectly against consulting firms and other information providers, including electronic and print media companies, some of which may have greater financial information-gathering and marketing resources than we do. These indirect competitors could also choose to compete directly with us in the future.*
>
> *In addition, limited barriers to entry exist in the markets in which we do business. As a result, additional new competitors may emerge and existing competitors may start to provide additional or complementary services. Additionally, technological advances may provide increased competition from a variety of sources."*

This topic is something I want to address, because there are a number of people who predict that Gartner can be replaced by a more informal and open rating system, and one that may even be free.

Gartner Versus Bottom-up / Crowdsourcing Alternatives

Some people have proposed that the analysis that Gartner performs could be supplanted by lower cost alternatives. As Barbara Tarallo states:

> *"There used to be a time when the first place technology buyers would go to for product information was Research firms. I think many technology vendors today are moving away from the 'pay to play' engagement, and part of the reason is that it's cost prohibitive in this economy for the smaller vendors to rate well no matter how innovative their technology. While analyst research provides an invaluable service to the marketplace for technology vendors, I think the analyst's role is beginning to change as more and more technology buyers are turning to social networking sites (like LinkedIn) to find new IT solutions. These social forums allow them to share challenges with their peers and get recommendations on how to deal with them. I think more and more analysts are taking on a validation role rather than a predictor role in the technology market. Social media networks are providing information on the latest trends and the analysts are confirming the players."*

This is a very interesting observation and a number of people have made similar observations/predictions. The first point regarding how difficult it is for smaller vendors to rate well no matter how innovative their technology, is something I already agreed with before reading this quote from Barbara Tarallo and something which I demonstrated in Chapter 5: "The Magic Quadrant." What Barbara Tarallo is referring to here is called "crowdsourcing." (*The practice of obtaining needed services, ideas or content by soliciting contributions from larger groups of people, and especially from an online community rather than from traditional employees or suppliers.*—Merriam Webster Dictionary) However, I very much doubt social networking sites like LinkedIn or other crowdsourcing sites can supplant an analyst firm such as Gartner. I cannot recall being on a project and having someone quote LinkedIn or other sites as a reference for software. Intrigued by Barbara's comment, I performed a number of searches in LinkedIn using different software selection questions, and did not find LinkedIn to have very much content on this topic. These sites have been around for some time; if they have not developed as competitors to Gartner up to this point, why should they in the future? Furthermore, I have visited other sites where people offer opinions on the software that is my expertise, and I have found many opinions offered that seem to have to do with how a product can be used hypothetically, rather than how it is used in reality. Quite a few individuals seem to be willing to restate some vendor's marketing material, but have never actually configured the software or gotten it to work in the way they described. And of course, vendors and consultants are also on these sites, so there can be many issues regarding objectivity.

So while Barbara has good points on the problems that smaller vendors have in getting rated accurately with Gartner, it's hard to see any social networking site that has the ability to influence executive decision makers, but I do agree that these types of information/interchange sites exist in many other spheres. Furthermore, Gartner's entire operating approach is based upon an expensive model. Much of what Gartner does could be moved online and performed at far lower cost. Gartner's interaction approach is not only expensive for Gartner but is expensive in terms of the costs it imposes on vendors. So Gartner is certainly susceptible to competition based upon price, but Gartner is under little price pressure. Also, simply a lower cost option would have to jump a number of hurdles. Corporations are actually not that price sensitive with respect to this type of information. Gartner's costs are nowhere near the prices they charge and extremely high margins have not negatively affected their business.

Executive decision makers will always look for a credible entity that can provide recommendations on the software vendors in the categories that they are interested in purchasing, and for now at least, this is a position that is Gartner's to lose. Certainly we are moving to where local services for everything ranging from pizza parlors to dentists are rated on Yelp. A reliable crowdsourcing site or set of sites for enterprise software does have the potential to improve software selection decisions.

How Gartner is Very Well Positioned for the Future

Gartner greatly solidified its position through acquisitions. And certainly other analysis firms such as Forrester and Aberdeen exist. However, none have such a broad coverage of technology as Gartner and none are as close to as influential. There is, however, a threat to Gartner, but it is not listed in their annual report and it is not one that I have ever seen articulated in any of the research that I performed for this book. That threat is a combination of vendors putting their applications in the Cloud and making them available to buyers for testing directly over the Internet.

While infrequently discussed, Gartner's power stems in part from the fact that the software buyer cannot directly experience enterprise software; therefore, Gartner serves as a powerful middleman between buyers, investors, and the software applications and vendors. In just a moment I will get into how this could change in the future and what it could mean to Gartner, but in brief, Gartner's services could change such that they cease to rate vendors, rate hardware and services only, and simply report on trends in the technology marketplace. In doing so, Gartner would lose most of its consulting practice and the rates it could charge would decline steeply.

Gartner helps to perpetuate software selection along elitist lines, which is also consistent with how large companies make decisions. However, this is only one particular modality of decision making. Technology can be used to decentralize decision making and most appropriately to move the decision making—or at least provide some voting power—to the place in the organization where individuals with the domain expertise can make the decision. Executives should not care that much about making software selection decisions; they should care about making the *best* software selection decisions. Making the best software selection decision means getting the best software, which would mean getting more input from a wider circle of people in the company and abandoning the more isolated process of software selection currently used. There is an excellent vendor that offers a glimpse into this opportunity. This vendor is called Arena Solutions, and is a company I profiled in my book *The Bill of Material in Excel, Planning, ERP and PLM/BMMS Software*.

Arena Solutions makes bill of material management software. Arena is a multitenant SaaS/Cloud solution, and they provide anyone with the ability to test drive their software right on line if they request a free 30-day trial. At one time I logged in quite frequently to Arena Solutions to do everything from learn the application to take screen shots for the book I was writing. However, if I wanted to find out what was new I could get a new demo password from them and see what had changed for myself. This approach is still quite rare, but it has advantages for the software vendor in that interested parties can learn about the software on their own time without engaging in a longer-term and expensive sales process. It costs very little for Arena to make this trial available to companies, and reduces their sales costs.

Another vendor that does this is Fishbowl. Fishbowl makes several different applications, and allows them to be downloaded for 30-day trials. It should be no surprise that Fishbowl, like Arena, is a strong application that is easy to use, and that stands on its own. The vendors trust their customers to use the applications on their own, without attempting to control the entire process.

SalesForce.com is another excellent example. Salesforce has developed well-known CRM software, but has also created a platform where companies can connect an enormous number of applications, referred to as PaaS, or Platform as a Service.

> "As an organization, you also no longer have to build this component ERP landscape on your own. Software vendors are beginning to provide this component solution framework for you. Force.com (by SalesForce) is one provider taking a lead with this approach. On the Force.com platform, a company can subscribe to the financials component, and then choose to go with the Glovia OM or the Rootstock manufacturing component based on the company's needs."—To ERP or Not ERP, That Is the C Level Question

App exchange at SalesForce is based upon an open system where applications are added as if they are plugging into the SalesForce system. Roughly 1,500 applications are available on this exchange.

Rootstock Software® installation request

☑ **I have read and agree to the** terms and conditions .

At the Force.com website (managed by SalesForce), a huge variety of applications can be installed and tested before being purchased. The site manages integration. This allows a company to create a custom solution architecture for itself based upon testing, rather than based upon what one vendor has to offer or going through the sales process.

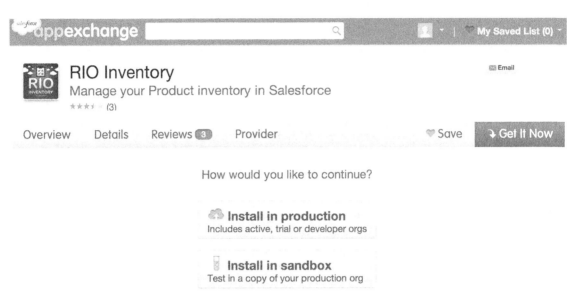

As shown above, in order to test this application, it could be installed on the sandbox created by SalesForce. This is the testing environment. If the company likes the application, they can install it on their production Force.com environment.

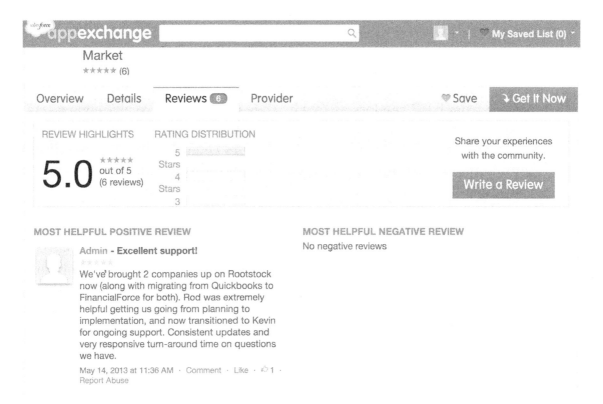

Force.com also has reviews of applications right in the app exchange. Shopping for applications like this is light years ahead of how it is currently done. SalesForce has basically brought the concept of Apple's AppStore to the enterprise software market.

So what if applications were available for a test right online as demo environments? What happens to Gartner? Gartner's power would decline because one needs less of an interpreter when experiencing the software first hand. But this still would not completely disintermediate Gartner for the following reasons:

1. This approach could only answer some of a buyer's product-related questions about an application category. For instance it would not answer broader questions for which Gartner provides analysis.

2. Few of the applications I work in can really be used in the way that Arena Solutions can—without special training. Applications would have to *be improved so that people can simply start using them without all of the normal overhead* such as training. I have heard all manner of excuses from ERP vendors as to why they refuse to make available a trial version of their software. Some argue that the software requires too much work to configure; however, potential buyers could log into a generic configuration. For instance, consultants like myself sometimes rent access to a managed application that is not maintained by any client. Yes, the system often has a lot of data entered by other users, but it is still extremely useful to always have a test system to access. The vendors of applications that are more difficult to use are not going to want to provide a test system because they know their applications will not perform well. Arena Solutions does not seem to have that problem because their software is logical and straightforward to use.

There is no denying that Gartner's power and authority rest upon the fact that buyers cannot directly experience the software that they want to purchase. Everyone is free to make their own prediction, but I don't think this situation will continue into the future. We are installing on-premises applications, customizing them, and then upgrading thousands of copies of these applications in what amounts to a job program for consultants and other infrastructure resources, and in doing so, we are passing along high costs to the buying companies and locking them in to the vendors that they choose. They are unable to sample applications before they use them, leading to poorer decisions than if they had had the opportunity to test-drive the applications.

The on-premises model currently being followed is antiquated, but still has legs. Vendors still have a ways to go in standardizing and improving the quality of the SaaS/Cloud model. For example, Force.com is not an open platform, but is still biased in favor of SalesForce (hardly a surprise). In addition, Force.com does not have enough meaty applications. Buyers have a long way to go to become familiar with this completely different operating modality. However, at some point, the SalesForce.com "model" will trump the SAP/Oracle "model" and when that happens, it will happen very quickly. I keep up with a variety of vendors and most of them are developing a SaaS version of their applications. Applications will then be easy to test and easy to install, and there will be a tipping point where most applications will be SaaS based and those that do not have a SaaS application will be considered out of touch. When this occurs, Gartner will no longer be the gatekeeper to what software should be used by companies. On the other hand, Gartner will not just sit by as they have their business model threatened; they will reconfigure themselves. Smart groups of people at Gartner have already figured this all out. Gartner is not the only company that will have to adjust; the software marketing function will be completely transformed under this new configuration, as second-hand information will mean less in the determination of software selection than it means under the on-premises model. The effect of SaaS/ Cloud on improving software selection has not been explored much as a theme by writers when comparing the costs and benefits of on-premises versus SaaS/Cloud.

Conclusion

Crowdsourcing alternatives sound appealing, but while this type of online ecosystem does a good job of pulling in opinions from many sources, it also has a number of weaknesses. Secondly, if these sites were to become more popular, vendor sales and marketing people from vendors would spend more time looking through them and inserting biased information into the discussions—something that already happens. If one were to imagine something like Wikipedia for enterprise software, the moderation challenge of such a site, with so much money on the line regarding how software is rated, would be a difficult challenge to manage. So far no site of this type provides the detailed analysis that Gartner and other IT analysts do. Gartner knows what its customers want and is very good at keeping their finger on the pulse of customers and providing them the type of information that they need. Criticisms of Gartner in this book are more around their transparency, but their marketing and their overall management of their business is difficult to critique. In fact, I consider Gartner's most impressive attribute to not be its research products, but instead its marketing and branding. Gartner provides the type of credibility that corporate decisions makers want and need. No one wants to be held responsible for a purchase without having said they consulted with some credible experts in the area. In fact, the greatest threat to Gartner is not other IT analyst firms but is the coming rise of SaaS. This is because SaaS will partially undermine Gartner's position as an information intermediary as obtaining first hand experience with online applications will become near universal and a standard way of finding information about applications. However, even under those conditions, I am confident that Gartner will find a way to adapt. Gartner is very well-positioned to influence enterprise technology purchasing and investing decisions for years to come—until the on-premises model of managing software is phased out. In the shorter term, I do not see evidence that executive decision makers are basing their short list upon a prominent source of media—crowdsourcing. Furthermore, executives are concerned with making good software selections, but more important to them is job security. They need to be able to point to someone with prominence who supports their selection decision. Pointing to LinkedIn is just not going to cut the mustard. Therefore, while cloud-based enterprise applications and vendors that offer free trials of their software online have the potential to somewhat reduce the power of Gartner, it does not eliminate the market for advice, particularly on the broader topics of enterprise software decision making.

CHAPTER 8

Adjusting the Magic Quadrant

As stated in Chapter 2: "An Overview of Gartner" as well as in various points throughout this book, in many cases Gartner's analysis cannot be used properly without adjusting the research output. By most analysts' accounts, only about twenty percent of the research that Gartner performs actually gets into a report. While Gartner publishes reports, it prefers to deliver more information by having clients consult with analysts. The downside to this, of course, is that consulting is more expensive.

Much of this book was dedicated to providing the background necessary for the reader to understand why Gartner reports must be adjusted. Companies can, of course, contact Gartner and ask questions, but at a cost. There are some things that can be adjusted without contacting Gartner, and some things that cannot. I have included some of the most common adjustments, and have listed those items that would require a company to contact Gartner to get more information.

Gartner Report Adjustment Rules

Never Use Just the Gartner Magic Quadrant to Make a Purchasing Decision

This point should be self-evident, especially if you have read the rest of the book up to this point. According to Louis Columbus, *"IT buyers regrettably sometimes make their entire purchasing decision just on the Quadrant alone."* It is hard to know where to begin as there are so many reasons not to do this, but as I have explained, Gartner's methodology for their Magic Quadrants includes factors that have nothing to do with the benefit to enterprise software buyers. Instead, the criteria are metrics that could be used by investors contemplating buying the software vendor's stock. Secondly, even Gartner does not want buyers or investors making decisions based simply upon the Magic Quadrant or any other research they produce. One should consider the research produced by Gartner as a "starter kit" to start the ball rolling for more analysis, contracting with Gartner for more analyst services, etc.

Adjust the Rankings for the Vendor's Size

Gartner prefers large software vendors. This large vendor orientation is clear, and it is difficult to see how a person doing a complete analysis on this topic could find that this bias does not exist. I hope that the analysis from Chapter 5: "The Magic Quadrant" has made that clear.

On the web there are several statements by Gartner analysts that Gartner does *not* favor large vendors. Other than managing perception, I can't think of a single good reason for anyone to say this. To believe that Gartner does not favor large vendors, one would have to both not understand the various Gartner methodologies and not read the Gartner research output.

A vendor's size is not a universal positive. Bigger vendors are less responsive, particularly if the buyer is not a large client. Because bigger vendors offer a broader set of products, they are constantly trying to capture more and more footprint within their existing clients, and they are not going to be happy selling a single application to a client. Larger vendors are less focused on their products, less focused on R&D, and more focused on marketing and on their partnerships with major consulting companies.

One of the reasons I enjoy keeping up with smaller best-of-breed vendors is because they have less bureaucracy, and they engage in far more innovation than the big vendors. I implement the software of the large vendors, and when I visit smaller vendors, I always feel as if I have traveled forward in time because the approaches we follow in SAP are so dated. I essentially implement approaches and technologies that are little changed from the mid-1990s. And of course, bigger vendors are more expensive (see the section on Adjusting for Price on page 126).

So, the bigger vendors in any Magic Quadrant are simply overrated by Gartner. The best way to account for this is by reducing their rating although I cannot provide a specific percentage adjustment.

Insert More Reality into Gartner's Ratings

Generally speaking, Gartner analysts do not have hands-on experience with the applications they are rating. Most of the Gartner analysts have at least fifteen years of experience in their area, so it is not that they lack experience but they usually lack implementation experience. Gartner analysts do speak with people in companies that implement software, but they speak at the level of CIOs and vice presidents. This constant interaction with senior executives at companies that buy enterprise software is a main reason why working for Gartner is considered to be such a good place to create contacts for future careers. However, these high-level people do not use the applications that they purchase; they pass along information to Gartner analysts that is already second-hand! While executives at buyers certainly know the problems that they face on implementations, overseeing implementations and actually working with the software are two different things.

Steps to Increase Reality of the Software Selection

Now that we have established that Gartner's ratings require more reality, the question is "how." An effective software selection will combine the high-level analysis provided by Gartner (provided either by reading research or by interacting with Gartner analysts) with more detailed analysis of:

- How the application actually works

- How the employees of the company will actually use the application

- How it will be configured and fit in with the rest of the company's footprint

Unfortunately, this is a lot more work and cannot be done by those who are the decision makers for the software selection. So, this more detailed work tends not to get done. However, it should be done—if not for all the applications under consideration then at the very least for the applications that the company finds the most intriguing. This applies to both buyers and investors, and is accomplished by having technical resources participate in the software selection process. I have no idea why so many executives think they are qualified to analyze statements made by presales consultants, but usually presentations are made to buyers with no one in the meeting from the buyer's side who can validate the technical statements made by the vendor's representatives.

Finding Technical Fact Checkers
Many times individuals with technical backgrounds can be pulled from the buyer's IT department. However, this is not always the case, especially if there is no one familiar with the category of application being analyzed. In Appendix A, I include a section on hiring independent consultants who can provide expertise that may not be available inside your company.

Viewing demos that are performed by a vendor's most skilled presales consultants is not a good way to truly understand an application. Rather than scripted demos, a more reality-based approach is to allow the reviewers to ask more questions and drive more of the demo. I cover this topic in more detail in the book *Enterprise Software Selection*.

Adjust Down the Rate of Predicted Change
As discussed in Chapter 2: "An Overview of Gartner," Gartner tends to overestimate the amount of change that occurs in any one software category, as well as the business developments in that category. Also, Gartner will describe industry trends as being more legitimate and permanent than they actually are. For instance, in my area, many companies have initiatives to move toward a make-to-order environment; however, because of the limitations of the approach most never will. This falls under the category of a "pipe dream."

It's easy to get the impression that because Gartner learns about these initiatives from senior executives within the buying companies, Gartner tends to take their word for it that most of these initiatives will succeed, when in fact a higher percentage may fail. This dynamic applies equally on both the buyer and the vendor side, as Gartner will frequently get on-board with a new technology initiative before a vendor and before that initiative has had the time to prove itself. For instance, in my field Gartner has been a major proponent of something called SAP Hana.[16] However, while the volume of the talk about Hana has been turned up for several years, I have yet to see its effect on any of my projects. I do not want to digress, as this is a separate and technical topic, but SAP Hana is really just something SAP should be doing anyway without a massive marketing offensive. It is simply a way to leverage evolving hardware and database technologies, and is really no big deal. In fact, I am surprised SAP and other vendors have not provided these options years earlier, as I began leveraging them myself on my own hardware several years ago. As I have stated previously, very little innovation happens at large software vendors. Small vendors put in the R&D and take the risk, and the large vendors copy the technology and crank up the marketing volume. When you control your customer base and have relationships with large consulting companies that recommend your product no matter its utility to their clients, innovation is simply not necessary. This is discussed in detail in the following link:

http://www.scmfocus.com/enterprisesoftwarepolicy/2012/03/11/why-the-largest-enterprise-software-companies-have-no-reason-to-innovate/

I have witnessed several innovations that no IT analyst firm has written anything about (one of which I covered in the book *Supply Chain Forecasting Software*). After a large firm has copied the technology, I assume I will read about how great it is in a Gartner report, maybe five years from now. In any case Gartner jumped on the Hana bandwagon while it was simply an experimental product. If Hana were released from a smaller vendor, it is highly unlikely that it would have been promoted by Gartner.

---

[16] The technology behind Hana is a huge yawn. It amounts to using solid state devices and new database structures that can handle very large data sets, and leverages SAP's database acquisitions to lock out Oracle from its accounts. In terms of the technology, these are things SAP should be doing anyway. A few years ago I ordered a laptop with a solid state drive because computers run better on them. I have also assembled multiple solid state drives in benchmarking tests of a planning system. However, I did not take out a press release after I did this. There are other areas of Hana that are adjustments to the database design and allow for faster table access. These are primarily for improving reporting speed.

As I hope the previous example demonstrates, Gartner is well-known for its Hype Cycle analysis, but Gartner itself will help drive a Hype Cycle to the "Peak of Inflated Expectations" (using Gartner's own Hype Cycle terminology). Often they are more swayed by how much "sense" a vendor's explanation seems to be over how it actually works in practice. Unfortunately, a lot of things seem like a good idea or seem to make sense but don't necessarily take flight. For example, SaaS was supposed to be the next great thing, but its adoption has been slow. Hypothetically, Gartner's frequent interaction with buyers should enable them to keep from doing this. However, my research into their past reports indicate that this is a consistent theme of Gartner despite their access to buyers that would allow them to validate vendors' statements.

Therefore, Gartner's reports should be adjusted and deferred. Whatever Gartner is predicting, it almost certainly will not happen as quickly as predicted. It should be understood that while many buyers may be moving in a particular direction, many will not be successful. Many initiatives are simply trends, and when they peter out, they are renamed. In my area, there is an initiative referred to as "lean," a rebranding of many identical initiatives of JIT (just in time), which mostly flamed out back in the 1980s. Lean is already running its course, and after it is not longer sellable, the consultants will come up with a new name for the same philosophies. There are now roughly half a million books on "lean," but the actual impact on inventory management?[17] Negligible. The benefit to consulting revenues of consultancies promoting lean concepts? Priceless.

Likewise, vendors frequently bring out new ideas and products, but most of these developments tend to be transitory and some are really just rebranding of old concepts by sales and marketing. Secondly, beyond time-phasing Gartner's predictions, many of their projections will never come to pass. When reviewing Gartner's past predictions, I found this repeatedly. Gartner's Hype Cycle proposes a consistent and eventual movement of technologies to the "Plateau of Productivity." However, some technologies or ideas are never implemented broadly and many disappear all together.

---

[17] Yes, I am joking. However, it is one of the most popular topics for publication in the supply chain management and production management space.

When No Magic Quadrant Exists

One of the biggest obstacles that a buyer or analyst can face is when there is no Magic Quadrant for the software category of interest. When Gartner decides to create a Magic Quadrant for a group of products or a software suite, it is impossible for a company, which only makes a single product, to compete in that type of analysis. Secondly, it is generally inadvisable for a buyer to implement multiple products from one suite. Doing this means using a vendor's weak products along with its stronger products, and in fact is the primary way that bad products are able to get sold. Without a connection to an ERP system, or as part of a suite, it is much more difficult for a bad product to get purchased. Also, once the analysis moves to the suite level, the business tends to get the short end of the stick, because at that point it simply becomes more about integration, and the functionality becomes an afterthought.

Nevertheless, software suites has been a common approach to IT implementation for several decades. While the concept was that there would be fewer integration issues if software suites were implemented, this approach has not meant the reduction in integration costs that were promised by ERP systems. This is explained in my book *The Real Story Behind ERP: Separating Fact from Fiction*.

Furthermore, this has meant that the business does not get the software it needs. Software selection based on software suites does not emphasize each application, but instead emphasizes the suite. As explained in this quote from Christopher Koch of *CIO Magazine*, software suites themselves are mechanisms that reduce the competition a vendor must face.

> *"Indeed, integration standards interfere with ERP vendors'*
> *traditional ways of gaining and keeping customers and market share.*
> *Before the Web came along, your integration strategy was simple: Buy*
> *as many pre integrated applications from a single vendor as possible.*
> *That worked for you, and it worked extremely well for the vendor;*
> *integrated application suites fetched a high price and required long-*
> *term maintenance and support contracts that promised a steady,*
> *predictable stream of revenue from customers."*—ABCs of ERP

I have now seen many poor-performing applications implemented and a great deal of frustration on the part of business users and managers who were not delivered applications that ever had a chance of meeting their requirements. Such high-level Magic Quadrants are not useful to a company that is selecting an application that is a subcategory of that Magic Quadrant.

If a company is looking to select one or multiple products from a suite, it's difficult to see how a high-level Magic Quadrant of this type can be adjusted. Some detail about specific applications can be provided in the vendor description section, but this is simply not enough detail to support an informed decision. At this point, the Gartner analyst must be contacted, and there is little value that can be received from the Magic Quadrant by itself.

Adjusting for Functionality and Maintainability

Gartner employs analysts with a strong tendency to look at the bigger (biggest?) possible picture. Gartner looks at so many factors outside of how good the application actually is and how maintainable the solution is, that these most important factors are under-emphasized. Corporate buyers should strive to obtain the software that closely matches their business requirements and has the very best functionality. Gartner essentially tells buyers that the application is really just one component to the decision, but the problem is that Gartner has too many factors pulling their ratings away from practical software implementation criteria. This can be addressed by checking reference accounts and by asking the Gartner analyst how the various vendors performed on the surveys for functionality and maintainability.

Disregarding Gartner's Deeper Technology Insights and Predictions

In their reports, Gartner will sometimes make technology projections or try to describe the technology. I have found quite a few of these statements to be unreliable. Gartner shows no evidence of being predictive; there is no reason to pay attention to their predictions.[18] Furthermore, Gartner's technology prediction opinions have been lampooned in numerous articles on the Internet, by authors

---

[18] Gartner acquired a prominent IT analyst firm that specialized in my software category: AMR Research. Not only was AMR Research sometimes wrong, AMR was spectacularly wrong as I explain in this article: http://www.scmfocus.com/scmhistory/2010/07/how-analysts-got-everything-wrong-on-marketplaces/

who are experts in that particular category of technology. A number of the technology predictions I have read seem to have been designed to create a splash, rather than to stand the test of time. One that definitely sticks out as ludicrous was the prediction by Gartner that the Windows Phone would become the second most popular smartphone platform between 2012 and 2015 and account for 19.5% market share. 2015 is not yet upon us, but the Windows Phone has only 3.2% market share. Another example is taken from their prediction on SaaS, which is a quotation I also used in Chapter 2.

> *"'Up until now, the unique nature of the software market has meant that buyers had very little negotiating power after the initial purchase of a software license,' Gartner Vice President William Snyder said in a research note. 'We expect those dynamics to change considerably over the next 5 to 10 years, giving CIOs and software procurement officers more bargaining power while potentially reducing software vendor profit margins."*

> *"Gartner also predicts that a fourth of all new business software will be delivered by software as a service by 2011'."*

Software costs have not significantly declined as predicted by Gartner. Gartner also overshot their second prediction that a fourth of all software would be delivered as SaaS by 2011. As of 2012, software delivered by SaaS represents only four percent of total software sales. Granted, SaaS software is less expensive than on-premises software, so the number of seats served is no doubt higher than its sales percentage. But it's difficult to see how the delivery of SaaS as a percentage of all enterprise software would be anywhere close to the twenty-five percent value of software delivery estimated by Gartner.

Was this bad analysis on the part of Gartner? Based upon the enormous advantages that SaaS has in terms of cost and time to deploy, as well as the efficiency of central administration by the vendor, I believe Gartner's projections were reasonable at the time. However, what many people who predicted a faster growth failed to consider were issues ranging from security concerns to the lower customizability of SaaS solutions, as well as the perception of integration issues that prevented SaaS from taking off as initially expected. The fact of the matter is that technology prediction is a difficult business. However, Gartner is not correct enough of the time for it to be taken seriously. Gartner has not demonstrated any special aptitude for technology prediction. On the other hand, if your client base does not notice Gartner's prediction track record, and if the bold predictions make for good marketing copy, then I suppose there is no reason to stop.

For those looking for technology predictions, Forrester has a better reputation for being right than Gartner.

Adjusting for Price

As was discussed in Chapter 5: "The Magic Quadrant," Gartner does not account for price in their rankings. Instead they compare all products as if they are in the same cost category. This approach creates a bias toward more expensive products. In addition, because Gartner's methodology ranks larger vendors higher, Gartner's recommendations tend to push buyers to higher-priced products and products that result in higher consulting costs. (Larger vendors tend to have both higher acquisition costs and higher consulting costs.) Therefore, it makes the most sense to adjust Gartner's ratings for price. Unfortunately, this is not an easy task.

There are few software vendors like Arena Solutions and Demand Works that post the cost of their software on their websites. In fact, in many years working in the field of software implementation, I am rarely informed of the actual costs of the software being installed. Many vendors are cagey about their price; among a host of factors, the price depends upon the number of seats and how much the software vendor wants the account. Determining the actual costs is time consuming and requires a significant amount of interaction with the software vendor so they can "understand their requirements."

Gartner is perfectly positioned to provide some type of rough approximation of the cost of the software, which could allow buyers to put some vendors out of their cost range. They are also well-positioned to estimate the consulting/implementation and maintenance costs of the different vendors per software category. However, if a company does not want to use a Gartner analyst to answer these questions, the company can adjust for Gartner's large vendor bias (and by extension their bias toward expensive solutions bias). They can push a smaller vendor up in consideration in order to account for lower cost and better value, if of course the vendor has other compelling factors. This leads to the next area of adjustment.

Adjusting for the Buying Company's Size

Gartner's bias toward larger vendors is related partially to Gartner's belief that companies prefer (or should prefer) to buy from the largest vendors. However, while larger buyers may prefer to purchase from larger vendors, it is less true of smaller buyers. Of course, Gartner's largest customers are the biggest companies in the world.

I do not know if smaller buyers would prefer buying from larger buyers if they could afford to do so, but the fact is that smaller buyers often can't. Generally small innovative vendors offer point solutions, have small deal sizes, and sell to small buyers. As the vendor grows, it is able to increase the size of buyers to which it sells. Therefore, Gartner's ratings fit the preferences (and checkbook) of large buyers far more than they do for smaller companies. Experience over time will let the smaller buyer know who they can afford to buy from, so for smaller buyers it is a simple matter to remove all or the majority of the largest vendors from their list and to focus on the other vendors.

Conclusion

While Gartner publishes reports, companies that buy subscriptions receive only a small percentage of their research. In order to maximize their revenues they prefer to deliver more information by having clients consult with analysts. The downside to this of course is that consulting is more expensive. This chapter is designed to prepare buyers to work in a more cost effective manner with Gartner. One should consider the research produced by Gartner as a "starter kit" to start the ball rolling for more analysis, contracting with Gartner for more analyst services, etc. Gartner's research can be adjusted by adjusting downward the rankings for the larger vendors, as they are inflated. Secondly, as an implementer myself, Gartner's research often makes me uncomfortable because it is at such a high level. In the software categories that are my areas of expertise the analyst writing the report clearly does not have enough hands-on experience to explain the reality of the implementation issues that will be faced during the implementation, and a consultation with the analyst is not going to change their knowledge level. Gartner does a nice job of using surveys to uncover implementation challenges faced by clients with different software, but even still, this does not adequately find its way back into the Magic Quadrant ratings as my example of the highly problematic SAP BW product should demonstrate. This chapter explained how to add more reality into the software selection process, and I consider this to be one of the most important parts of software selection. Adjusting down the predicted rate of change is necessary because Gartner tends to overestimate this in their analysis. Initiatives are frequently announced with great fanfare, but most of them fail to find any purchase within organizations. Executives both overestimate the degree of innovation occurring within their own companies, and are naturally persuasive individuals, which is a major reason they have the positions that they do. Gartner often appears to be drinking the Kool-Aid that is served by the buyers they interview. However, there is an optimism bias as the executives will always be confident of new initiatives within the company. Gartner's Kool-Aid drinking extends to vendors as well, particularly large vendors.

Another area that must be adjusted is functionality and maintainability. Gartner underestimates the importance of both of these dimensions of software implementation. The functionality is critical to the ROI and probability of success of the implementation. Because Gartner underemphasizes functionality, it has the consequence of promoting the purchase of riskier applications. In terms of maintainability, Gartner had clear evidence of the maintenance problems with SAP BW, yet they continued to list SAP in the Leader Quadrant. Certainly, the fact that SAP is the largest business intelligence software vendor makes them a "leader" in terms of their market share—and this is of course quite important to investors, however, its unclear how simply having a large market share helps an application be maintained by a buyer. If the lowest quality offering, an application with very significant implementation and maintainability issues can be listed in the Leader Quadrant, then Gartner's Magic Quadrant must be adjusted by buyers because these dimensions are of more importance to the buyer than they are being weighted by Gartner. The price of applications must be adjusted for by buyers. Gartner does not rate either the actual application cost, nor the TCO in the Magic Quadrant, so the most expensive solutions are placed on equal footing with the least expensive. However, the price is important to buyers and therefore, looking at a Magic Quadrant without adding price into the equation would not make much sense.

CHAPTER 9

Is Gartner Worth the Investment?

Is Gartner Worth the Investment for Investors?

This question of value is the easiest to answer for investors, so I have placed it first in this chapter. This question is so easy to answer because there is probably no group whose interests are as well-served by Gartner's research than investors.

I would not be the first to argue that Gartner's research is more relevant for investors than it is for software buyers. But this also depends upon what analytical product is being used by the investor.

1. Investors can be confident that right or wrong, Gartner's opinions will be considered definitive by a large segment of the people that can have a powerful effect on a vendor's future condition. Because buyers have to actually implement the application and gain value from its operation, *buyers cannot be as confident.* So while perception is reality for investors, this not true for buyers. For example, when I see a bad application rated highly in a Gartner Magic Quadrant, investors can be confident that the product will be included in the short lists of many software selections, so perception in effect becomes reality. Strangely, while

Gartner's research seems skewed toward investors, according to Gartner investors only represent roughly five percent of all business, at least by number (not by revenue).

2. If investors seek to use Gartner for its technology or market predictions, there is no evidence that Gartner can forecast better than anyone else. Due to famous misses, it seems that in some cases (at least according to anecdotal evidence) Gartner is not even attempting to achieve forecast accuracy, but is attempting to either make a splash with a prediction or satisfy a large vendor with its projections.

A standard and very basic subscription to Gartner begins at roughly $30,000, but there are rumors that a subscription can be had for less if all that is required is online access to the article database and very limited questions for analysts. The less a company pays, the less access they have to Gartner analysts.

Investing Based Upon Gartner's Ratings

As I stated in Chapter 2: "An Overview of Gartner," I am convinced that a number of studies of the effect of Gartner's Magic Quadrant on the stock performance of software vendors have been performed and that a positive correlation has been found. These studies will never be revealed and will be used to improve the performance of the technology fund that performed the analysis. Most likely the studies that have been performed privately have not only charted the increased stock price brought about by a favorable rating, but address the conditions under which a favorable rating has the most effect (most likely when the rating of a medium-sized vendor increases significantly from the previous year's Magic Quadrant). The ideal vendor would match up well with Gartner's Magic Quadrant methodology; however, they should be concentrated in that Magic Quadrant. A large vendor that competes in multiple Magic Quadrants would be more difficult to track because they may have improved their position in some Magic Quadrants, or stayed the same or even declined in others.

An investing company would need to review the Magic Quadrant as soon as it is published and make their buying decision as soon as they can before others are able to do the same. That is, they would need to determine their investing strategy and be ready to trade before the fact. There are at least two "plays" available to the investment company. One is the longer-term play that the vendor will receive more sales because of their enhanced Gartner rating, and the second is the short-term play that other investors (and possibly insiders at Gartner) are also savvy to the relationship and are buying the same stock.

According to my interviews with Gartner, investors are not all that focused on the Magic Quadrant. Often investors are looking for the next big thing. They want to know who is innovating. In addition to reading Gartner research and talking to analysts, investors can also attend various networking events.

Is Gartner Worth the Investment for Software Buyers?

The answer to whether Gartner is worth the investment for buyers depends upon a number of factors. For instance, one important variable is how much is spent. Some buyers only purchase a subscription from Gartner, while other buyers spend upward of $10 million on Gartner, at least in some years.

My observation, which is supported by many others who have analyzed this issue, is that far too often software buyers take Gartner's reports at face value and focus too much on the results without reviewing the context. (There is also an open question as to how thoroughly executives actually read the Gartner reports.) Gartner clearly does not want buyers to use their analytical products without paying to discuss the products further with an analyst. In terms of getting the best value for the time spent with a Gartner analyst, I would recommend simply telling the analyst your high-level requirements and then letting them recommend a short list of vendors for you. A full Gartner-guided software selection will be quite expensive and not entirely necessary.

The Gartner analyst is not the best person to tell you if a vendor can meet your specific requirements. That is why I recommend communicating your high-level requirements to the analyst. Analysts at Gartner do not get into that level of detail in their vendor briefings. Standard types of information to have ready prior to such a call with a Gartner analyst would be:

1. How much you want to spend

   2. Your general preferences :
      a. Are you very focused on having leading functionality, or on having a
         low risk implementation?
      b. How important is software support to you?
      c. Etc.

   3. Where is the software being implemented now and in the future globally?

These are just examples; the Gartner analyst will have the full list of items that they will need in order to provide you with the feedback that you require. In addition to detailed surveys, the Gartner analyst will have their interactions with vendors and software demonstrations to work from. They will not release all of the survey information to you, but if you tell the analyst the type of information above, they can offer you a short list of vendors that may be a good fit for you.

Staying Away from Shortcuts
Many buyers will take shortcuts during the software selection process, and many are far too easily led through the process by skillful salespeople and presales people.[19] Under these circumstances, Gartner can do more harm than good. In fact, over-relying on Gartner analytical products—without getting context from Gartner—can cost a company far more than their subscription, and has cost a number of companies in exactly this way.

While we are on the subject of costs, a software buyer that has just a few purchases to make in a year will often need to spend at least $100,000 per year on Gartner once the analyst services are included.[20] This is not very much money for most enterprise software buyers, and if spending this money enabled better decision-making on just a single application selection, it would easily pay for itself. Every new software (or hardware, consulting, or telecommunications) purchase that is made, requires at least some type of advisement session with a Gartner analyst, and the more products to be purchased, the higher the cost. However, this price must also be compared against other alternatives in the market. Gartner may be able to provide actionable intelligence to buyers, but it is certainly not the only

---

[19] I cover this in detail in the book *Enterprise Software Selection*.
[20] Gartner has a number of buyers that spend over $10 million per year on their products and services.

source of information out there. In addition to asking the question of whether or not Gartner's research and discussions with analysts can improve software selection, the question must also be asked as to how Gartner's costs compare to alternative sources of information. More than likely Gartner is the most expensive information source that a company can purchase, so a little bit of Gartner buys a lot of information from other sources. I will get into this topic in more detail in the conclusion of this chapter, because it applies to all the categories of Gartner customers.

Is Gartner Worth the Investment for Software Vendors?

The first question of whether it is worth having a subscription to Gartner if one is a software vendor is generally a no-brainer, and the major vendors all know this and spend quite a bit of money on Gartner. Smaller vendors need to see where they rank, and the information that buyers and investors are reading about them.[21]

In addition to vendor ratings, Gartner offers a great deal of analysis regarding current topics in the software industry, with mergers or new directions for software, hardware and consulting companies. Even if a vendor disagreed with all of Gartner's ratings (and their own rating with Gartner), a subscription to Gartner would be valuable from the perspective of market intelligence.

Vendors *do* want to know the answer to one main question: whether Gartner is worth participating with in a more meaningful and expensive way (educating, buying consulting services from, attending Gartner events, etc.).

Any vendor who has dealt with Gartner knows how expensive it is to participate with them. How much it benefits a software vendor is very much based upon the nature of the vendor and their product. Of course it's more than that. A software vendor that is dedicated to improving its rating with Gartner must also invest time and energy into educating Gartner. It is estimated to cost between $50,000 and $100,000 in direct fees to keep Gartner up on one's products in a way that can put the vendor in the best possible position in the Magic Quadrant

---

[21] All that is known is what the large companies are reputed to spend, in addition to statements from different heads of marketing at vendors as to what they spent previously. I found from one source that IBM pays $5 million to Gartner, but I have no way of corroborating the source. It is generally estimated that the major vendors are all in the multi-million dollar range.

and in Gartner's other analytical products. This is sometimes referred to as the "Gartner Tax." There are numerous approximations of how much it costs to get your software rated with Gartner, and so much of it is situational. There is also the question of how many products a vendor has to offer. This initial estimate is for one or two products. The price does not scale directly with each new product that the vendor needs to educate Gartner about, but generally the price does go up. Because many of the cost estimates are not specific as to the number of products for which Gartner is providing technology advisor services, the exact amount of money a vendor would need to budget is not known. Some interesting quotes on this topic are listed below:

> *"...the cost of creating a good relationship with a Gartner Group analyst seems to average around $75K."*—Anonymous on Quora.com

> *"Being a client enables you to get 'face time' with the Gartner analyst team which is critical to getting their mindshare and more favorable positioning for you. This means attending their events and scheduling 1-on-1 time with them regularly, responding to all their requests for information and even booking a few days of paid analyst consulting time.*

> *"(You can start off at a minimum) for $25K but if you want to really get value out of it you will want to spend more. Factoring in travel costs and extra fees it's probably closer to $50–100K/year for a full effort."*—Kris Tuttle, Director of Research, Soundview Technology

The quotations above are instructive regarding the costs to vendors to hire Gartner, and their cost estimates are similar. However, I want to note that these are only the explicit or direct costs of hiring Gartner. There are also internal costs that a vendor must tabulate in order to calculate their total costs. For example, not included in these costs estimates is the vendor's labor cost to comply with Gartner's requirements. There are forms to be filled out and communication with Gartner to keep up. A software vendor might make a similar investment when trying to make a software deal. The difference is that there is no software sale at the end of the process, only the potential that future customers will contact the software vendor because of the better ranking provided by Gartner. A vendor can easily recover that much in software sales and consulting fees that would result from an improved Gartner rating.

There is no reason as to why dealing with Gartner should cost this much, except that Gartner is in a dominant position in the IT analyst space, and therefore vendors can expect to have to play by their rules. Gartner can demand a premium payment from software vendors, and many software vendors are obligated to pay it.

Part of this money is spent on marketing types, generally referred to as analyst relations, who know how to speak Gartner's language—or what Gartner calls being "Gartnered." Gartner analysts want to feel important and are compensated partially based upon how much consulting services they initiate. This should not be surprising, because consulting generally works this same way. Gartner analysts often state on public forums that they do not know which vendors are contributing; however, this can't be true. Part of the system is not only the money, but also the positive reinforcement that the analyst receives from being hired for their expertise by the vendor. Again, it is nothing new that people tend to be positively predisposed toward those who enhance their career and treat them well. This is another reason why the more technology advisement services the vendor purchases the more they can enhance their rating. This is explained by the quotation below:

> *"In addition to consulting services, there is a cost to participate in Gartner conferences, which start at roughly $35,000 for the basic package (booth at a conference, Gartner-arranged private get-together with potential clients, etc.), and can move up rapidly in price."*

I have broken down the benefits by vendor size in the following paragraphs.

For Large Vendors

For the major software vendors, the benefits they receive from Gartner is quite substantial and the decision to participate is an easy one. I am certainly not telling large vendors anything they don't already know. Furthermore, large companies like SAP, Oracle and Microsoft have so much money, what is several million handed over to Gartner? Gartner's methodologies are designed to make these large vendors look as good as possible, so the value to these vendors is excellent and they all sign up for Gartner's services.

I have read Gartner statements where they say that software buyers are increasingly interested in future solutions under development by major vendors. As a result, major vendors are being listed in quadrants for which Gartner readily admits the vendor has no product—yet. The value in doing so is to get software buyers to postpone their software selection until a major software vendor they are familiar with comes out with the application.

For the major vendors, Gartner is just one of several strategies that allow them to not have to compete as much on their product, which include partnering with major consulting companies, promoting the integration of applications within their suites, etc.

Furthermore, SAP, Oracle, IBM and Microsoft are able to outspend (in time and money) smaller vendors and get higher ratings that are especially valuable for marginal or immature products. For instance, any new product that SAP comes out with, no matter how buggy, will be rated decently simply because of SAP's size. Microsoft SharePoint, the worst content management system I have ever seen, but one that I am forced to use because it is installed at every one of my clients, is actually well-rated by Gartner.

Gartner seems to rate large software vendors high on "ability to execute," even when I have seen many implementation problems, so being big is no guarantee of implementation success. Gartner does survey on quality measurements, but the methodology—just being large—increases how Gartner views a vendor's "ability to execute." This category of vendors doesn't really need to invest much time impressing Gartner, and for big vendors, Gartner is an automatic purchase. For all of these reasons the large vendors are perpetual Gartner customers in the realm of multi-million dollars per year.

For Medium-sized Vendors
For medium vendors, the marketing benefit to improving or maintaining one's quadrant position/rating is typically worth the yearly cost and associated costs of

working with Gartner. This is particularly true of vendors that have international offices and broader software suites, and therefore fit with Gartner's methodologies. I believe the benefits are clearly fewer for medium-sized vendors, but the return on investment can still be positive.

For Small Vendors

Chapter 5: "The Magic Quadrant" demonstrated that in Gartner's rating system, the smaller the vendor, the more difficult it is to score well. Small vendors may have the best products in their class, but the best they can hope for is to make it into the Visionary quadrant, and that is if they are lucky enough to compete in a Magic Quadrant specifically directed toward their product rather than a Magic Quadrant where their product must compete against software suites.

Gartner salespeople will make the pitch that buying their consulting services can improve a vendor's ranking, but given their criteria, it's more sales talk than reality, because it does not fit with Gartner's methodology. I have pointed this out previously, but it's worth repeating: I do not think that Gartner will adjust the numbers for a vendor that pays them money and purchases their technology advisor services. Rather, the methodology, combined with higher exposure to products from vendors that they are paid to get to know better, is where the improvements in rankings come from.

To give smaller vendors that don't really have a chance of doing well in the Magic Quadrant the incentive to buy consulting services, Gartner may profile them as a "Cool Vendor," which is another report that they create. This prevents Gartner from losing revenue due to smaller vendors dropping out.

> *"First of all there are so many different quadrants at this point (so that competing firms can each claim a top spot) that virtually anyone can claim that they are in the upper right. Secondly, what CFO will base their decision on what Gartner says? Every firm has a unique 'Magic Quadrant' based on their history, infrastructure, existing portfolio, etc. To suggest that there is a universal winner is simply marketing/revenue generation and a way for them to drive additional consulting services."*—Jon Carrow

However, in the final analysis, no other Gartner product is close to as influential as the Magic Quadrant. (I asked this question of people I interviewed for this book, and they could not recall other Gartner analytical products as being that influential.) I do not recall people adding the winners of "Cool Vendors" to a software selection short list.

If a vendor's product is well-known in its space, Gartner will want to include it in the Magic Quadrant regardless of whether the vendor pays Gartner or not. However, they won't rank the vendor where it should be ranked because of the criteria they use. Many small vendors who repeatedly see larger vendors with worse products than theirs ranked significantly above them in the Magic Quadrant, typically opt out of the Gartner system once they find out how much money Gartner wants for their services. The smallest vendors with the most innovative products tend to take the dimmest view of Gartner's research. Secondly, smaller software vendors have less money to spend than the larger software vendors. Therefore, participation and consulting services purchased from Gartner is much less of a sure thing. However, Gartner can begin to make sense to a small vendor depending upon the timing and where that vendor is in their growth stage, as well as how neatly their products fit into the Magic Quadrant. For example, smaller companies that are ready to make the next move and that have the organizational and consulting capabilities to handle larger deals, may feel it is time to engage Gartner.

Obviously, there are not just three categories of vendors (large, medium, small) but rather a continuum of vendors. The bigger you are as a vendor the more incentive there is to participate with Gartner.

Conclusion

Gartner has three major customer bases and this chapter analyzed the value to each of these types of customers in buying subscriptions and consulting services from Gartner.

Vendors receive the best value from Gartner because Gartner's orientation is much more toward the investment potential of a software vendor than the factors that are important to buyers—which is counterintuitive when you consider that buyers are the largest of Gartner's customer bases. As for buyers, the estimation of the value of a Gartner subscription or paying to be consulted by Gartner analysts is complicated by a number of factors. Even when speaking with the analyst, Gartner lacks the practical implementation experience or software background with the applications it reviews that would make their advice more accurate and valuable. Other complicating factors are that many buyers misuse Gartner's analytical products by not checking the methodology, and Gartner can become a crutch, where the executive essentially gives up their responsibility to perform a thorough software selection and put the work in, and instead rely upon Gartner, which provides them with an easy answer. In this way, Gartner simply becomes a mechanism for justifying following the herd, regardless of the applicability of the application or even the application category to the buying company. Furthermore, Gartner is, in many cases, merely purchased and referenced for political cover—and its actual research value essentially meaningless. That is, the executive requires an external entity with credibility to bless an application, so they can make the purchase without assuming any personal risk. When this is the case, the use of Gartner's analytical products will result in a worse decision than if Gartner's analytical products and services were never used.

The value for software, hardware and even service vendors is a much more straightforward affair and the value is strongly related to how large the entity is that is making the decision. For large vendors the decision is automatic and the value is quite significant. With large payments to Gartner for "technology advisory services," the vendor's positioning of their applications, regardless of their degree of innovation, maintainability, implement ability, or the other factors important to buyers is more or less a sure thing. For small vendors the decision is also straightforward, for them Gartner is a poor value. The question becomes a bit more murky when the vendor is midsized.

CHAPTER 10

Conclusion

This book did not analyze every one of Gartner's analytical products, but instead focused on the value related to software and vendor rankings. There are a number of additional services that can be purchased from Gartner. For instance, some companies hire Gartner to help them raise money from the investment community. I did not analyze and cannot say how much Gartner charges for this service or what their success ratio is for assisting companies in raising capital.

Chapter 4: "Comparing Gartner to *Consumer Reports*, the RAND Corporation, and Academic Research," explained that while Gartner markets itself as a research company, it does not actually follow most of the rules of research. This should give Gartner's customers pause, particularly because of what is known about the money Gartner receives from vendors in technology advisement services. Gartner's Office of the Ombudsman is unconvincing as a mechanism for addressing the inherent conflicts of interest that exist that are a feature of how Gartner markets its products and services to both buyers and sellers. This is because the Gartner Ombudsman does not conform to any of the standards that are generally accepted of an ombudsman in other areas where the role of an ombudsman also exists. The Gartner

Ombudsman may declare the impartiality of Gartner in a continuous fashion, but these statements does not constitute evidence.

For those that choose to use Gartner, it is important to understand the methodology of their various analytical products. For example, even the Niche Player category of the Magic Quadrant, which appears to be the lowest ranking possible within this analytical product, is not being used to dissuade companies from buying that application—and this is according to Gartner. Gartner analytical products often leave one conflicted because while they appear to quantify the scoring of a vendor in a particular application category. However, the more one investigates the methodology of the analytical product and the more one speaks with Gartner analysts, the less the products seem to say what they initially appear to say. The Gartner analytical products like the Magic Quadrant have a number of easily demonstrated biases. Buyers that intend to use the Magic Quadrant would make a major error in not adjusting the Magic Quadrant for these biases, and exactly which biases these are and the importance of adjusting for them was previously discussed.

Comparing Gartner research to the alternatives, such as other IT analyst firms, must also be addressed. For instance, even though Gartner is much larger and more prominent than Forrester, there are some things that Forrester simply does better. If the focus is content management and collaboration software (and more), The Real Story has far less financial bias than Gartner because they do not take money from vendors. Depending upon the specific category of software, there may be a smaller IT analyst firm that covers it better. As usual, the best approach is not to commit everything to one IT analyst firm, but to use different ones for different purposes. One strategy might be to purchase multiple-seat Gartner subscriptions, but only use Gartner analysts for the software categories where Gartner is the preferred source, and to augment Gartner with other IT analyst firms for specific software categories where these firms have better offerings. Unlike Gartner, many IT analyst firms allow their customers to buy a single article, making for a very cost effective approach and allowing the company to compare and contrast different reports.

However, other IT analyst firms are not the only alternative to Gartner. For instance, I rely often upon academic research when writing books and articles. Academic research will not tell you if you should buy vendor A or vendor B, but provides a good overview of software categories. Another reason to look for a diversity of opinion beyond IT analysts is that writing orientation is completely different. For instance, as with consultants, all IT analysts tend to be promotional because they make money when companies buy and implement new software. Academic researchers simply want to get more funding to perform more research; they are not attempting to sell software or consulting services. As a result, academic research is not promotional, and may provide a historical context often missing from commercial information sources.

Aside from the orientation of the writing, the depth of analysis is another reason to expand outside of IT analysts and general IT publications. Academics are trained to thoroughly research the nature of cause and effect. All academic research is performed by individuals with PhDs, so there are more highly-trained researchers in academia than exist in IT analyst firms (although some of those that work in IT analyst firms do have PhDs). Academic researchers perform literature reviews, and make sure that their research conclusions are consistent, or that any discrepancies can be explained within the context of other research in the same area. Academic research is of course less up-to-date than IT analyst research, so one cannot expect the latest happenings in IT from academia. All this to say that IT analysts should only be seen as one potential information source for a company that wishes to inform its decision-making.

The final point is that IT analyst research is the most expensive of the various written sources of information available to a company. The money spent on a certain level of IT analyst research can purchase an enormous amount of information from other sources. Of course, this scenario changes a bit depending upon the party using the information. Vendors wanting to improve their ranking with Gartner will need to spend money on Gartner's technology advisor services, and then make the adjustments recommended by Gartner. But buyers and investors should first determine how much time and money is to be allocated to software research. IT analysts should be allocated some percentage of that total, and within that category, Gartner would be a certain percentage.

As you can see, I am suggesting that companies develop a research strategy that takes into account all the different sources of information available to the company and that justifies how much time and money is to be spent on each information source. All of the various information sources have sliding scales in terms of time and effort. Performing such an analysis will likely lead to the best value for a company's research effort. By studying a wider view of the overall research effort, one can make the appropriate trade-offs. However, by and large, the major customers for Gartner's research do not do this (with the exception of investors who are quite used to synthesizing various information sources). Buyers tend to go directly to Gartner or to their other favorite IT analyst firm when a purchase decision is pending. Oftentimes the decision of who to rely upon is ad hoc and based simply upon what the company did in the past.

How to Use Independent Consultants for Software Selection

One of the biggest mistakes made by executive decision makers is that more often than not they go into interactions with software vendors without technical resources to advise them. While some executive decision makers may have worked in software at some point, the typical executive—at least in US corporations—is not up on technology. Decisions on information technology purchases are most often made by representatives of the part of the business that will use the application (for instance, the finance department for financial software) along with IT. However, being a bit distant from the technology is also true of executive decision makers that work in IT, such as the CIO and Vice Presidents. At that level the work is much more abstract, focused more on budgets and making the numbers work than technology.

When software vendors perform demos or otherwise provide information to executives, they make a number of contentions about the technology that the executives are not in the best position to verify. Secondly, as the prospective buying company does not own the software, technical resources internal to the company are most often not in the best position to verify the software vendor's claims. Usually a consulting firm will not provide the necessary information because of the bias of consulting firms as was described in Chapter 3: "How to Use Consulting Advice on Software Selection" in my book *Enterprise Software Selection*.

The best-case scenario is to find an independent consultant through something like LinkedIn. Independent consultants who have experience in the application can be hired and can verify statements made by the software vendor. However, a few rules should be followed to ensure that you control for bias as much as possible.

1. When the independent consultant is hired, be clear that the consultant will only participate in the software selection phase. If the independent consultant believes that he or she may gain more work after the selection, you run the risk of biasing the independent consultant in favor of a particular software vendor so that they can then work on the implementation.

2. When searching for an independent consultant, it's important to find one that has exposure to several applications in the area so that he or she can compare and contrast the different applications for you. During software selection, multiple companies present to the prospect, and the independent consultant that you choose should be familiar with several of these applications.

3. During the interview with the independent consultant, determine if they can see the positives and negatives of the applications that they will be helping you evaluate. If they are cheerleaders for one application, they will not be able to help you even if they are quite knowledgeable about the technology.

4. Independent consultants move from project to project. Software selection projects, because they are shorter, are not as desirable as implementations, which are much longer contracts. You cannot expect an independent consultant to be available exactly when you want to review software vendors. However, you can hire independent consultants part time and remotely, meaning that they educate you remotely, listen in through a conference call, view the demo through a web conference, and review the material given to you remotely. This remote approach is quite a bit more cost-effective and

most independent consultants would be amenable to this arrangement. On the other hand, if the independent consultant is available to work full time, there are advantages in that the consultant can provide you with a general education about the software category and can help structure the analysis for the software selection. In many cases, executive decision makers are busy attending meetings or with other operational tasks, and employing someone who can really concentrate on the software selection can provide benefits.

Of course, problems arise when no independent consultant can be found with experience in the particular software, as is sometimes the case with smaller applications where the independent consulting market is simply not well-developed. In these situations, the best that can be done is to find an independent consultant with similar experience and exposure.

Other Books from SCM Focus

Bill of Materials in Excel, ERP, Planning and PLM/BMMS Software

http://www.scmfocus.com/scmfocuspress/the-software-approaches-for-improving-your-bill-of-materials-book/

Constrained Supply and Production Planning with SAP APO

http://www.scmfocus.com/scmfocuspress/select-a-book/constrained-supply-and-production-planning-in-sap-apo/

Enterprise Software Risk: Controlling the Main Risk Factors on IT Projects

http://www.scmfocus.com/scmfocuspress/it-decision-making-books/enterprise-software-project-risk-management/

Enterprise Software Selection: How to Pinpoint the Perfect Software Solution using Multiple Information Sources

http://www.scmfocus.com/scmfocuspress/it-decision-making-books/enterprise-software-selection/

Enterprise Software TCO: Calculating and Using Total Cost of Ownership for Decision Making

http://www.scmfocus.com/scmfocuspress/it-decision-making-books/enterprise-software-tco/

Gartner and the Magic Quadrant: A Guide for Buyers, Vendors, Investors

http://www.scmfocus.com/scmfocuspress/it-decision-making-books/gartner-and-the-magic-quadrant/

Inventory Optimization and Multi-Echelon Planning Software

http://www.scmfocus.com/scmfocuspress/supply-books/the-inventory-optimization-and-multi-echelon-software-book/

Multi Method Supply Planning in SAP APO

http://www.scmfocus.com/scmfocuspress/select-a-book/multi-method-supply-planning-in-sap-apo/

Planning Horizons, Calendars and Timings in SAP APO

http://www.scmfocus.com/scmfocuspress/select-a-book/planning-horizons-calendars-and-timings-in-sap-apo/

Process Industry Planning Software: Manufacturing Processes and Software

http://www.scmfocus.com/scmfocuspress/production-books/process-industry-planning/

Replacing Big ERP: Breaking the Big ERP Habit with Best of Breed Applications at a Fraction of the Cost

http://www.scmfocus.com/scmfocuspress/erp-books/replacing-erp/

Setting up the Supply Network in SAP APO

http://www.scmfocus.com/scmfocuspress/select-a-book/setting-up-the-supply-network-in-sap-apo/

SuperPlant: Creating a Nimble Manufacturing Enterprise with Adaptive Planning

http://www.scmfocus.com/scmfocuspress/production-books/the-superplant-concept/

Supply Chain Forecasting Software

http://www.scmfocus.com/scmfocuspress/the-statistical-and-consensus-supply-chain-forecasting-software-book/

Supply Planning with MRP/DRP and APS Software

http://www.scmfocus.com/scmfocuspress/supply-books/the-supply-planning-with-mrpdrp-and-aps-software-book/

The Real Story Behind ERP: Separating Fact from Fiction

http://www.scmfocus.com/scmfocuspress/erp-books/the-real-story-behind-erp/

What Does the History of Media Tell Us About This Topic?

Historical media analysis tells us that media output tends to align with the interests of those who control it and pay for it. As an example, the primary reason that advertised television tends toward so much unchallenging programming is that challenging programing puts viewers in a critical mindset, making them less susceptible to advertising. The best programming to put viewers in the correct mindset for suggestibility is lighthearted fare.

Evidence that smoking advertisements lead to adjustments in the media's coverage of the dangers of smoking is now well-established. Smoking was at least suspected of causing cancer before the following ad ran in 1931, and yet ads like this, with doctors promoting certain brands, continued to run for decades after the industry knew the relationship by the late 1950s.[22] Cigarette advertising was shown to relate directly to the number of anti-smoking stories. In effect, for decades cigarette advertising slowed the dissemination of information about the real risks of smoking. The story repeats itself today as Exxon-Mobile has made contributions to the Heritage Foundation and the National Center for Policy Analysis (NCPA). Unsurprisingly, both entities have published "misleading and inaccurate information about climate change" according to Bob Ward, the policy director at the Grantham Research Institute on Climate Change and the Environment at the London School of Economics.

[22] *"Evidence linking smoking and cancer appeared in the 1920s. Between 1920 and 1940, a chemist named Angel Honorio Roffo published several articles showing that cancers could be experimentally induced by exposure to tars from burned tobacco. Roffo et al. further showed that cancer could be induced by using nicotine-free tobacco, which means that tar, with or without nicotine, was carcinogenic. Research implicating smoking as a cause of cancer began to mount during the 1950s, with several landmark publications in leading medical journals. The first official U.S. government statement on smoking and health was issued by the Surgeon General Leroy Burney in a televised press conference in 1957, wherein he reported that the scientific evidence supported cigarette smoking as a causative factor in the etiology of lung cancer."*

As pointed out by the Stanford School of Medicine, *"Unlike with celebrity and athlete endorsers, the doctors depicted were never specific individuals, because physicians who engaged in advertising would risk losing their license. It was contrary to accepted medical ethics at the time for doctors to advertise, but that did not deter tobacco companies from hiring handsome talent, dressing them up to look like throat specialists, and printing their photographs alongside health claims or spurious doctor survey results. These images always presented an idealized physician—wise, noble, and caring. This genre of ads regularly appeared in medical journals such as the* Journal of the American Medical Association, *an organization which for decades collaborated closely with the industry. The big push to document health hazards also did not appear until later."*

The paper *What Do the Papers Sell? The Model of Advertising and Media Bias*, as well as other papers on the influence of payments on media, demonstrates a consistent conclusion.

> *"The regulatory view grew out of evidence that some advertisers seriously interfere with media content. Baker (1994) and Bagdikian (2000) detailed accounts of the history of suppression of news on tobacco-related diseases. Complementing this evidence, Warner and Goldenhar (1989) statistically identify tobacco advertising as causing the reporting bias (for further evidence, see e.g., Kennedy and Bero, 1999). Another more recent case is misreporting on anthropogenic climate change. Boyko and Boyko (2004) demonstrate a clear bias in the US quality press over 1988-2002 (see Oreskes, 2004, on the scientific benchmark). Automotive advertising has been signaled as a key explanatory factor: in the US in 2006, automotive advertising alone accounted for $19.8 billion, of which nearly 40% went to newspapers and magazines."* —Advertising Age, 2007

So there are consistent findings in other media outlets that payments from subjects influence editorial content. More observations can be found in the well-known paper (in media analysis circles at least) *Do Ads Influence Editors? Advertising and Bias in the Financial Media:*

> *"For their part, media outlets tend to strongly deny that such a pro-adviser bias exists. For example, a 1996 article in Kiplinger's*

*Personal Finance printed statements from editors at a number of personal finance publications (including the three in our study) claiming that advertisers have no influence over published content. In this paper, we test for advertising bias within the financial media. Specifically, we study mutual fund recommendations published between January 1997 and December 2002 in five of the top six recipients of mutual fund advertising dollars. Controlling for observable fund characteristics and total family advertising expenditures, we document a positive correlation between a family's lagged advertising expenditures and the probability that its funds are recommended in each of the personal finance publications in our sample (*Money Magazine, Kiplinger's Personal Finance, and SmartMoney). *While we consider several alternative explanations below, the robustness of the correlation leads us to conclude that the most plausible explanation is the causal one, namely, that personal finance publications bias their recommendations—either consciously or subconsciously—to favor advertisers."*

Advertising affects editorial decisions; this is a clear and unequivocal finding.[23]

---

[23] With some uncommon candor, a French TV executive opened up about the actual purpose of his television channel. *"[French TV channel] TF1's job is to help a company like Coca-Cola sell its products. For a TV commercial's message to get through, the viewer's brain must be receptive. Our programs are there to make it receptive, that is to say to divert and relax viewers between two commercials. What we are selling to Coca-Cola is human brain time."* What is surprising to most people who buy magazines is that they are not the only "payer" for the product. The consumer buys and pays for the magazine at the newsstand; however, advertisers pay in effect to have the magazine produced. The percentages of overall revenues are shown in the following quotation. *"Mainstream US newspapers generally earn over 50 and up to 80% of their revenue from advertising; in Europe, this percentage lies between 30 and 80%, e.g., averaging 40% in the UK (see e.g., Baker, 1994; Gabszewicz et al., 2001). Overall, advertising exceeds 2% of GDP in the US and a substantial fraction of this becomes media revenue: 17.7% to newspapers, 17.5% to broadcast TV, 7.4% to radio and 4.6% to consumer magazines."* What Do the Papers Sell? The Model of Advertising and Media Bias, *Advertising Age, 2007.*

In this way, many media outlets can be seen to have two customer bases: their audience and their advertisers. That is, they receive income from both the buy and sell side. This is similar to Gartner. However, because advertisers are much more concentrated, advertisers have even more power than the percentage of revenue they contribute to the media outlet. For instance, one member of the audience cannot seek to influence the media product. In fact even ten percent of the audience would not be effective in influencing the media output; audience members do not coordinate with one another so their influence is diffused. However, a single advertiser can influence the media product, and the larger the advertiser the more its ability to influence the media entity.

This issue is not merely restricted to companies that create ratings, but to all forms of media. Media outlets that are completely independent financially from those that they report on have a much better ability—both in theory and in actuality—to stay independent from the industries that they cover. Prior to the stock market crash of 1929, many reporters for financial publications would take direct payments to write glowing reviews/predictions of stocks by financial manipulators. The manipulators would buy a number of shares at a low price, and then sell their shares as soon as the article came out. This was so common that it had a specific name: "pump and dump." Many similarly corrupt arrangements were behind many of the financial panics prior to and since 1929. The corruption of the general financial press and of rating agencies plays a decisive role in financial panics and in a small minority getting very wealthy. Having a prestigious brand name is no protection against corruption; in fact the most prestigious brands have the greatest ability to both drive and benefit from financial bubbles. Anyone who thinks that firms that do this will eventually be made to pay by the "market," only have to look as far as Moody's, Standard and Poor's, and Fitch—three rating agencies that rated billions of toxic assets as the highest investment grade. They are still doing very well, thank you very much. I have a side interest in economics, and what I have found is that the smaller media outlets that are less known and take in very little revenue consistently outperform the much larger media and better-known outlets that do take advertising. Very simply, money corrupts the media product.

Disclosure Statements and Code of Ethics

In addition to disclosing income sources (which Gartner does not do), relationships should be disclosed as well to provide the reader with the ability to understand the bias of the analyst or author. One of the best disclosure statements is from Phil Wainewright of ZDNet, and I have copied it below:

> *"Finally, as a matter of disclosure, I must add that some of these vendors, including NetSuite, SAP and Workday, are past or present consulting clients and often fund my travel to attend their events. Others brief me over lunch or dinner from time to time, and several work with me in the EuroCloud trade association. While they all know not to expect any favors from me in my independent writing, it's inevitable that a closer relationship means I'm more aware of their business than those of other vendors I speak to less frequently."*

National Public Radio

Disclosing and even recusing oneself from covering certain topics is part of a journalistic code of ethics. One example of this is the code of ethics of National Public Radio, which can be found at the following link:

http://ethics.npr.org/category/e-independence/

The following quotations from this code of ethics are relevant to the study of IT analysts:

> *"In general, we don't do outside work for government or agencies principally funded by a government, or for private organizations that are regularly covered by NPR. This includes work that would be done on leaves of absence.*
>
> *This means we don't ghostwrite or co-author articles or books or write reports—such as annual reports—for government agencies, institutions or businesses that we cover or are likely to cover. We may permit exceptions for activities that don't seem to pose a risk of undermining our credibility. Speaking to groups that might have a relationship to a subject that NPR may cover requires high-level approval; contact Ethics."*

The BBC

The BBC has the most extensive documentation on journalistic/editorial code of ethics that I have ever read. It can be read at the following link:

http://www.bbc.co.uk/guidelines/editorialguidelines/

I found the following quotations from the BBC code of ethics to be interesting and applicable to the content covered in this book:

> *"There must never be any suggestion that commercial, financial or other interests have influenced BBC editorial judgments. Those involved in the production of BBC content must have no significant*

connection with products, businesses or other organizations featured in that content."

"Regular BBC news presenters should not undertake promotions, endorsements or advertisements for any company, outside organization or political party. In exceptional circumstances, with the prior approval of the BBC, they may undertake promotional activities for books which they have written. Any such activity must not jeopardize a presenter's reputation for objectivity and impartiality."

The New York Times has a particularly detailed explanation of its code of ethics, which can be read at the following link:

http://www.nytco.com/press/ethics.html

References

Alexander, Raquel-Meyer. *Measuring Rates of Return for Lobbying Expenditures: An Empirical Case Study of Tax Breaks for Multinational Corporations.* April 10, 2009. http://papers.ssrn.com/sol3/papers.cfm?abstract_id=1375082.

Bandor, Michael S. *Quantitative Methods for Software Selection and Evaluation.* Carnegie Mellon University, 2006.

Bell Labs. Last Modified August 12, 2013. http://en.wikipedia.org/wiki/Bell_Labs.

Blumberg, Alex. *Forget Stocks Or Bonds, Invest In A Lobbyist.* January 06, 2012. http://www.npr.org/blogs/money/2012/01/06/144737864/forget-stocks-or-bonds-invest-in-a-lobbyist.

Boyer, Ken. *Behind the Scenes at Starbucks Supply Chain Operations: Its Plan, Source, Make & Deliver.* April 17, 2013. http://www.supplychain247.com/article/behind_the_scenes_at_starbucks_supply_chain_operations/green.

Burnson, Patrick. *Gartner's 2013 Ranking of "Top 25" Supply Chains Announced.* May 30, 2013. http://www.supplychain247.com/article/gartners_2013_ranking_of_top_25_supply_chains_announced/supply_chain.

Byrne, Tony. *Getting beyond the Magic Quadrant for WCM*. August 26, 2010. http://www.realstorygroup.com/Blog/1981-Getting-beyond-the-Magic-Quadrant-for-WCM.

Cameron, Preston D. *The Software Selection Questionnaire*. Phoenix Publishing Group, 2002.

Cold Fusion. Last Modified August 6, 2013. http://en.wikipedia.org/wiki/Cold_fusion.

Colquhoun, David. *Publish-or-perish: Peer review and the corruption of science*. The Guardian: September 5, 2011. http://www.theguardian.com/science/2011/sep/05/publish-perish-peer-review-science.

Columbus, Louis. *Gartner's Magic Quadrant May Need New Pixie Dust*. April 15, 2005. http://www.ecommercetimes.com/story/42302.html?wlc=1222636414.

Consumer Reports. Our Mission. http://www.consumerreports.org/cro/about-us/our-mission/index.htm.

Criticism of advertising. Last modified June 12, 2013. http://en.wikipedia.org/wiki/Criticism_of_advertising.

Crowdsourcing. Last modified July 29, 2013. http://en.wikipedia.org/wiki/Crowdsourcing.

Cummings, Michael et al. *The Cigarette Controversy*. December 15, 2006. http://cebp.aacrjournals.org/content/16/6/1070.long.

Dignan, Larry. *Microsoft leads slowing enterprise software market*. April 22, 2013. http://www.zdnet.com/microsoft-leads-slowing-enterprise-software-market-7000014344/.

Ellman, Matthew. *What do the Papers Sell?* March 2008. https://docs.google.com/viewer?url=http%3A%2F%2Fwww.iae.csic.es%2FinvestigatorsMaterial%2Fa8287092114archivoPdf1062.pdf.

Elmer-DeWitt, Philip. *The Best Analysis Money Can Buy*. October 8, 2009. http://tech.fortune.cnn.com/2009/10/08/the-best-analysis-money-can-buy/.

Enderle, Rob. *Can a New Analyst Firm Take Down Gartner?* May 11, 2012. http://www.cio.com/article/706262/Can_a_New_Analyst_Firm_Take_Down_Gartner_.

Evaluating research companies: Gartner, Forrester, and IDC. June 6, 2011. http://www.infrics.com/2011/06/evaluating-research-companies-gartner.html.

Evelson, Boris. *Top 10 BI Predictions For 2013 and Beyond*. December 12, 2012. http://blogs.forrester.com/boris_evelson/12-12-12-top_10_bi_predictions_for_2013_and_beyond.

Force. Last modified May 15, 2013. http://en.wikipedia.org/wiki/Force.com.

Francica, Joe. *Why Gartner's Magic Quadrant Missed the Importance of Location Analytics to Business Intelligence.* May 13, 2013. http://www.directionsmag .com/articles/why-gartners-magic-quadrant-missed-theimportance-of-location-analytic/326188.

Gareth Herschel and Matthew Goldman. *Getting "Gartnered": How Vendors Can Work With Gartner.* http://www.gartner.com/it/about/max_time/Getting_Gartnered_ How_Vendors_Can_Work_With_Gartner.pdf.

Gartner Annual Report, Gartner, 2012

Gartner Group. Last modified July 30, 2012. http://techrights.org/wiki/index.php/ Gartner_Group.

Gartner, Inc. *Contract Review.* http://www.gartner.com/technology/research/contract_ review.jsp.

Gartner, Inc. *Gartner Consulting.* http://www.gartner.com/technology/consulting/.

Gartner, Inc. *Gartner Guiding Principles.* http://www.gartner.com/it/about/omb_ guide2.jsp.

Gartner, Inc. *Gartner Industry Advisory Services.* http://www.gartner.com/it/products/ research/ias.jsp.

Gartner, Inc. *Gartner Research.* http://www.gartner.com/technology/research.jsp.

Gartner, Inc. *Gartner Says Worldwide Supply Chain Management Software Market Grew 12.3 Percent to Reach $7.7 Billion In 2011.* http://www.gartner.com/ newsroom/id/2016915.

Gartner, Inc. *Methodology.* http://www.gartner.com/technology/supply-chain/top25_ methodology.jsp

Gartner, Inc. *Peer Networking.* http://www.gartner.com/technology/research/peer_ networking.jsp.

Gartner, Inc. *Vendor Briefings.* http://www.gartner.com/it/about/vendor_briefings.jsp.

Gartner, Inc. *Why Gartner.* http://www.gartner.com/technology/why_gartner.jsp.

Goldacre, Ben. *Bad Pharma: Drug research riddled with half-truths, omissions, lies.* January 27, 2013. http://www.salon.com/2013/01/27/bad_pharma_drug_ research_riddled_with_half_truths_omissions_lies/.

Grantee Standards. July 2005. http://www.nsf.gov/pubs/manuals/gpm05_131/gpm5. jsp#510.

Gruman, Galen. *The Truth About Software as a Service.* May 21, 2007. http://www
.cio.com/article/109706/The_Truth_About_Software_as_a_Service_SaaS_.

Harris, Derrick. *Gartner Gets It Wrong With Cloud Quadrant.* January 4, 2011.
http://gigaom.com/2011/01/04/gartner-gets-it-wrong-with-cloud-quadrant/.

Hollander, Nathan. *A Guide to Software Package Evaluation and Selection: The
R2ISC Method.* AMACOM, 2000.

Hopkins, William. *Gartner buys AMR: What does it mean to YOU?* http://www
.knowledgecap.com/uploads/KCG/KCG%20on%20Gartner%20acquiring
%20AMR.pdf.

Howlett, Dennis. *Gartner in the dock over Magic Quadrant.* October 20, 2009.
http://www.zdnet.com/blog/howlett/gartner-in-the-dock-over-magic-quadrant/1424.

IMRAD. Last modified August 11, 2013. http://en.wikipedia.org/wiki/IMRAD.

Industry analyst. Last modified May 23, 2013. http://en.wikipedia.org/wiki/
Industry_analyst.

Johnston, Josephine. *Conflict of Interest in Biomedical World.* http://www
.thehastingscenter.org/Publications/BriefingBook/Detail.aspx?id=2156.

Kanaracus, Chris. *Gartner: Software as a Service Market to Grow 17.9 Percent to
$14.5 Billion.* March 27, 2012. http://www.pcworld.com/article/252658/gartner_
software_as_a_service_market_to_grow_179_percent_to_145_billion.html.

Koch, Christopher. *The ABCs of ERP: Getting Started with Enterprise Resource
Planning.* January 10, 2006. http://teaching.fec.anu.edu.au/INFS3024/
Lecture%20Notes/The%20ABCs%20of%20ERP%20-%20Enterprise%20-
%20CIOb.pdf.

Krieger, Lisa. *Stanford divided on tobacco dollars.* May 06, 2007. http://www.calstate
.edu/pa/clips2007/may/7may/stan.shtml.

Krugman, Paul. *Berating the Raters.* New York Times: April 25, 2010. http://www
.nytimes.com/2010/04/26/opinion/26krugman.html?_r=1&.

Magic Quadrant, Gartner, March 7 2013

Magic Quadrant. Last modified July 8, 2013. http://en.wikipedia.org/wiki/
Magic_Quadrant.

McCue, Andy. *Software-licensing costs predicted to fall.* November 19, 2007.
http://news.cnet.com/Software-licensing-costs-predicted-to-fall/2100-1011_
3-6219263.html?.

McLellan, Charles. *The Evolution of Enterprise Software: An overview.* May 1, 2013. http://www.zdnet.com/the-evolution-of-enterprise-software-an-overview-7000014006/.

McNeil, Taylor. *The Man Who Did the Math.* April 4, 2011. http://now.tufts.edu/articles/man-who-did-math.

Methodology. http://www.thefreedictionary.com/methodology.

Network Effect. Last modified August 12, 2013. http://en.wikipedia.org/wiki/Network_effect.

Obal, Philip. *Selecting Warehouse Software from WMS & ERP Providers, Expanded Edition: Find the Best Warehouse Module or Warehouse Management System.* Industrial Data & Information Inc., 2007.

Peer Review. Last modified August 3, 2013. http://en.wikipedia.org/wiki/Peer_review.

Pelz-Sharpe, Alan, *De-mystifying the Gartner ECM Magic Quadrant.* September 28, 2007. http://www.realstorygroup.com/Blog/1023-De-mystifying-the-Gartner-ECM-Magic-Quadrant.

Pressombudsmannen. Last modified March 15, 2013. http://en.wikipedia.org/wiki/Pressombudsmannen.

Principal–agent problem. Last modified August 6, 2013. https://en.wikipedia.org/wiki/Principal%E2%80%93agent_problem.

Protalinski, Emil. *Facebook accounts for 1 in every 5 pageviews.* February 2, 2012. http://www.zdnet.com/blog/facebook/facebook-accounts-for-1-in-every-5-pageviews/8491.

RAND Corporation. *Major Clients and Grantors.* http://www.rand.org/about/clients_grantors.html.

Reames, Patrick and Vasey, Dr. Gary M. *Selecting and Implementing Energy Trading, Transaction and Risk Management Software: A Primer.* BookSurge, 2008.

Relax News. *Brompton bike creator wins UK's longest-running design award.* The Independent: October 16, 2009. http://www.independent.co.uk/property/house-and-home/brompton-bike-creator-wins-uks-longestrunning-design-award-1804152.html.

Rich, Michael. *Perpetuating RAND's Tradition of High-Quality Research.* November 2011. http://www.rand.org/standards.html.

Rich, Michael. *Standards for High-Quality Research and Analysis.* http://www.rand.org/content/dam/rand/pubs/corporate_pubs/2012/RAND_CP413-2012-02.pdf.

Schaeffer, Chuck. *Truths When Selecting Supply Chain Management Software.* http://www.allsupplychain.com/supply-chain-software-fit.php.

Scherbina, Anna. *Analyst Disagreement, Forecast Bias and Stock Returns.* Harvard University, 2004.

Schestowitz, Roy. *Microsoft Corruption in Russia Helps Derail Migrations to GNU/Linux.* July 20, 2012. http://techrights.org/2012/07/20/.

Slywotzky, Adrian. *Where Have You Gone, Bell Labs?* August 27, 2009. http://www.businessweek.com/magazine/content/09_36/b4145036681619.htm.

Smith, Catharine. *Amazon's Top Reviewers: Who They Are and What They Do.* The Huffington Post: June 16, 2011. http://www.huffingtonpost.com/2011/06/16/amazon-top-customer-reviewers_n_878262.html?.

Snapp, Shaun. *Supply Chain Forecasting Software.* SCM Focus Press, 2012.

Social Media. Last modified August 10, 2013. http://en.wikipedia.org/wiki/Social_media.

Social Network. Last modified August 8, 2013. http://en.wikipedia.org/wiki/Social_network.

Tobacco Advertising Themes. http://tobacco.stanford.edu/tobacco_main/images.php?token2=fm_st003.php&token1=fm_img0111.php&theme_file=fm_mt001.php&theme_name=Doctors%20Smoking&subtheme_name=Throat%20Doctors.

Trebilcock, Bob. *Another Good Bounce.* July 2012. http://mmh.com/images/site/MMH1207_SpRpt_Top20Software.pdf.

UNHCR Internal Review. http://www.unhcr.org/pages/49f0619f6.html.

Vance, Ashlee. *NY Times rattles IT industry with analyst ban.* December 12, 2006. http://www.theregister.co.uk/2006/12/12/analyst_nytimes/.

Whitehorn, Mark. *Is Gartner's Magic Quadrant really magic?* March 31, 2007. http://www.theregister.co.uk/2007/03/31/myth_gartner_magic_quadrant/.

Whittaker, Zach. *Android accounts for 75 percent market share; Windows Phone leapfrogs BlackBerry.* May 16, 2013. http://www.zdnet.com/android-accounts-for-75-percent-market-share-windows-phone-leapfrogs-blackberry-7000015496/.

Will the industry analyst business be dead in five years? June 19, 2011. http://www.horsesforsources.com/analysts-survive_062011.

Winner of the 2006 Bogie for Achievement in Contrived Quality Surveys. http://web .archive.org/web/20070604152957/http://www.radaronline.com/features/2006/09/ jd_power_associates.php.

Xerox Alto. Last Modified August 12, 2011. http://en.wikipedia.org/wiki/Xerox_Alto.

Links in the Book

Chapter 1

http://www.scmfocus.com/scmfocuspress/it-decision-making-books/
gartner-and-the-magic-quadrant/

http://www.scmfocus.com

Chapter 3

http://www.gartner.com/it/about/vendor_briefings.jsp

Chapter 4

http://blogs.gartner.com/ombudsman/2012/12/11/important-
updates-to-gartner-external-use-policy/

http://www.gartner.com/technology/supply-chain/top25_
methodology.jsp

http://www.gartner.com/DisplayDocument?doc_cd=154752

http://www.cbs.nl/en-GB/menu/methoden/default.htm

Chapter 5

http://www.gartner.com/technology/research/methodologies/magicQuadrants.jsp

http://www.scmfocus.com/enterprisesoftwarepolicy/2012/03/11/
why-the-largest-enterprise-software-companies-have-no-reason-to-innovate/

http://www.scmfocus.com/enterprisesoftwarepolicy/2012/01/02/
why-ibm-should-not-be-allowed-to-acquire-software-companies/

http://www.scmfocus.com/enterprisesoftwarepolicy/2011/11/19/
the-case-against-sap-for-anti-trust-violations/

http://www.scmfocus.com/scmhistory/2013/06/
how-the-original-logic-fo-erp-systems-turned-out-to-be-false/

http://www.scmfocus.com/supplyplanning/2011/09/17/what-if-you-paid-nothing-
for-sap-software-how-saps-tco-compares-for-supply-planning/

http://www.scmfocus.com/productionplanningandscheduling/2011/08/09/what-
if-you-paid-nothing-for-sap-software-how-saps-tco-compares-for-production-
planning/

Chapter 6

http://www.netsuite.com/portal/press/releases/nlpr05-13-13.shtml?inid=gartner

Chapter 8

http://www.scmfocus.com/enterprisesoftwarepolicy/2012/03/11/
why-the-largest-enterprise-software-companies-have-no-reason-to-innovate/

http://www.scmfocus.com/scmhistory/2010/07/
how-analysts-got-everything-wrong-on-marketplaces/

Author Profile

Shaun Snapp is the Founder and Editor of SCM Focus. SCM Focus is one of the largest independent supply chain software analysis and educational sites on the Internet.

After working at several of the largest consulting companies and at i2 Technologies, he became an independent consultant and later started SCM Focus. He maintains a strong interest in comparative software design, and works both in SAP APO, as well as with a variety of best-of-breed supply chain planning vendors. His ongoing relationships with these vendors keep him on the cutting edge of emerging technology.

Primary Sources of Information and Writing Topics

Shaun writes about topics with which he has first-hand experience. These topics range from recovering problematic implementations, to system configuration, to socializing complex software and supply chain concepts in the areas of demand planning, supply planning and production planning.

More broadly, he writes on topics supportive of these applications, which include master data parameter management, integration, analytics, simulation and bill of material management systems. He covers management aspects of enterprise software ranging from software policy to handling consulting partners on SAP projects.

Shaun writes from an implementer's perspective and as a result he focuses on how software is actually used in practice rather than its hypothetical or "pure release note capabilities." Unlike many authors in enterprise software who keep their distance from discussing the realities of software implementation, he writes both on the problems as well as the successes of his software use. This gives him a distinctive voice in the field.

Secondary Sources of Information

In addition to project experience, Shaun's interest in academic literature is a secondary source of information for his books and articles. Intrigued with the historical perspective of supply chain software, much of his writing is influenced by his readings and research into how different categories of supply chain software developed, evolved, and finally became broadly used over time.

Covering the Latest Software Developments

Shaun is focused on supply chain software selections and implementation improvement through writing and consulting, bringing companies some of the newest technologies and methods. Some of the software developments that Shaun showcases at SCM Focus and in books at SCM Focus Press have yet to reach widespread adoption.

Education

Shaun has an undergraduate degree in business from the University of Hawaii, a Masters of Science in Maritime Management from the Maine Maritime Academy and a Masters of Science in Business Logistics from Penn State University. He has taught both logistics and SAP software.

Software Certifications
Shaun has been trained and/or certified in products from i2 Technologies, Servigistics, ToolsGroup and SAP (SD, DP, SNP, SPP, EWM).

Contact
Shaun can be contacted at: shaunsnapp@scmfocus.com.

Abbreviations

ERP—Enterprise Resource Planning

SaaS—Software as a Service

SAP BW—SAP Business Warehouse

TCO—Total Cost of Ownership

CPSIA information can be obtained
at www.ICGtesting.com
Printed in the USA
FSOW03n0252100316
17757FS